IN FROM THE

COLD

What I've Learned About Life, Love, and Letting Go!

Juliette McNeil

In from the Cold: What I've Learned About Life, Love, and Letting Go!

by Juliette McNeil

copyright ©2019 Juliette McNeil
ISBN: 978-1-950718-12-2
published by Kudu Publishing
cover design by Martijn van Tilborgh
cover photo by Rex Singleton Photography

In from the Cold is available in Amazon Kindle, Barnes & Noble Nook and Apple iBooks.

CONTENTS

DEDICATION

T HIS BOOK IS IN MEMORY of my mother, Vera Mae Carbin (1930-1962), who was taken from this world long before her time. Her love and compassion for all people left an everlasting impression on me. May God give her peace in heaven that she never found on earth.

ACKNOWLEDGMENTS

I AM GRATEFUL to the many people who have supported and inspired me in the writing of this book. My heartfelt thanks to Mrs. Diane Welburn for planting the seed of writing the story of my life. I especially thank my husband, James, for all of his hard work keeping me on task; without his support and encouragement, this project would not have been completed. I also thank my sisters Emma Mosely Brown and Sarah Lee Wright for helping me to fill in the blank spots where I was too young to remember some of the details.

INTRODUCTION

THERE ARE SOME seven hundred and fifty miles between Mulga, Alabama, and 1600 Pennsylvania Avenue in Washington, DC. The trip from the simple, ash-filmed miner's home in which I grew up to the spotless, elegant rooms of the White House is northeast through three states. It would take you about twelve hours to drive, and the best part of a month to walk.

For me, the journey was a little longer. There was around a half-century between the days when I ate off the bare wooden floor I'd had to scrub clean on my hands and knees, and the genteel afternoon teas hosted by First Lady Michelle Obama, where I was treated like a guest of honor.

Along the way, I experienced abuse and prejudice, resistance and rejection. But I also encountered encouragement and help, kindness and comfort. As I look back, I see how all those different experiences helped form and forge me.

As a result, today I enjoy a life I could never have dreamed of—though it is not without its challenges, of course. Perfection isn't possible in a broken world. But I have found happiness and fulfillment in ways that I did not think were possible as an unwanted small girl.

I share my story now not to draw attention to myself, but hopefully to encourage others who may, as I did as a child, long to know that they matter. With God's help, and that of others, I have been able to take the hard times I have faced and see them turned to good.

As you follow my journey, may you be inspired in your own, however bumpy it has been so far, to know that you can find your way to a better place.

CHAPTER ONE

THERE IS AN old saying that "a journey of a thousand miles begins with a single step." In my case, traveling the long road from Mulga, Alabama, to our nation's capital probably began with a single stepmother, though I did not realize it at the time.

She came to our house when she and Daddy married just three months after my mother's death. For a nine-year-old girl still struggling to come to terms with losing someone so important, so abruptly, it was a huge additional emotional adjustment.

My new stepmother loomed large in every way. Standing around only 5 ft. 4 in., she seemed to be equally wide, probably weighing almost 300 lb. Her presence would cast a dark shadow over my life for many years before I was able somehow to transform it from darkness into a light that pointed the way forward to something better.

To begin with, things weren't too bad. Perhaps my stepmother felt sorry for me, or maybe she just thought it would be a good idea to try to win me over. Though she had three sons from previous relationships, she had no girl of her own, so it could be I filled some kind of a need for her. My older sisters were less accepting of this newcomer in their home, so I was an easier target to try to woo.

I wouldn't say that she was motherly, but she had moments when she would make some effort to care, like combing my easily tangled hair. On occasions she would make me clothes; we didn't have the money to buy anything new. Other than for the times when I became her dress-up doll, however, for the most part I was treated with indifference.

That absence of concern and affection leaves a mark on a child's soul, certainly, but my stepmother's dismissive neutrality was to be preferred to what became her active mistreatment.

It began in earnest after my older half-sister, Barbara, and older sisters, Emma and Sarah, had fled the home, leaving just me and my younger brother, Frankie. And when my stepmother and my father had a daughter of their own, suddenly she no longer had need for a surrogate little girl. Instead, I became the subject of her displeasure and scorn. It was as if someone flipped a switch and every ounce of anger, sadness, and malice in her body was laser-focused on me.

I lived in a state of constant fear: instead of a child, I became a slave. My stepmother barked out an endless list of menial and tiring chores, and nothing less than perfection in their execution was tolerated. I would be awakened before dawn on school days to clean the house top to bottom—and then sent off without any breakfast.

I was required to wash our clothing by hand using an old rubbing board. Not only did I have to do our family laundry, I was also made to wash the clothes of her sons, who still lived with their grandmother in nearby Woodward. I also had to starch and iron their long-sleeved shirts. Later, when Daddy purchased a washing machine, my stepmother used it for their laundry but required me to continue doing mine by hand.

On Saturdays, when other kids were playing or spending quality time with their friends and families, I was on my knees, working on the floors. First I would have to use a butter knife to carefully scrape up the old wax from the floor and from between the indents on the panels. Then I would rub the wax paste hard into the wood and buff it to a real shine. Occasionally, Daddy would rent an electric buffer for me to use, but usually it was down to me, manually. It would take hours. My hands were rubbed raw, and my knees were constantly sore—to this day you can trace a faint blemish on them from all the time I spent kneeling.

There was one good thing about having to keep the floors in such good condition; it made having to eat my meals there less unpleasant. My stepmother and my father would dine at the table or sit in their easy chairs in the family room while we kids were forced to eat on the floor, like the family dog. The dining table was out of bounds for us because it had to be kept for special occasions, in which case we might make a mess— though we never had visitors to the house.

Despite all the mistreatment, I still sought out my stepmother's approval. Maybe I was motivated by fear of even worse treatment, or perhaps I was still desperate for the motherly role model every young girl needs, but I continued to work hard to make her happy. Though I was sore and tired from the long hours of manual labor that she forced upon me, I would then volunteer to do additional work around the house. I also assisted her at her job cleaning a local doctor's office. Somehow I kept hoping that just as the switch had flipped one day and made her so cruel, perhaps I'd unlock the key to making her nice again. But no matter how much I tried, my stepmother's dark eyes never lightened.

If anything, her presence became even more monstrous. She seemed to take some sort of perverse pleasure in being spiteful. She no longer took the time to help me with my hair, though she knew how important it was to me. I would ask her repeatedly, but she would usually refuse. Every few weeks she would relent and help me try to tease my hair into some sort of shape. On rare occasions, she would drive me to school, but usually I had to get there and back on foot. My high school was a little over three miles from home, and I had to be back by 3:30 p.m. to begin my afternoon chores, so I would have to run all the way to avoid getting into trouble. That meant I was never able to participate in extra-curricular activities, which only further isolated me from all the other kids.

When I began my menstrual cycle, she did not buy me sanitary napkins to keep clean. At a time when a girl most needs a safe harbor, I was left to face this emotional and developmental storm on my own. I had to find whatever I could to keep from soiling myself: I'd use old rags, toilet tissue, and paper towels. It's remarkable that I didn't develop any physical problems, but the scarring of my heart was immense.

Even in the face of all this, something in me yearned for her tenderness. One evening in my teen years I made the mistake of telling my stepmother that I wished we could have a close relationship like my friends had with their mothers. While no one in our community was wealthy, I'd seen friends' moms take them out shopping and spend time with them. I craved that sort of attention and guidance, but telling my stepmother that was a huge mistake. She took it as a criticism.

When my father got home from work that evening, my stepmother stunned me with an unbelievable lie.

She told him that I had wanted her to talk with me about boys and sex. While I was certainly curious about the opposite sex by this time, and even had a puppy-love crush on a boy in my class, I was far too shy and introverted to ever raise such a topic. When Daddy came and asked me about it all, I was mortified.

Overwhelmed with embarrassment, I fell to the floor, which he took as some kind of sign. "You fell because you are guilty!" he boomed, standing over me and berating me as I remained frozen and humiliated. I'd taken my share of whippings from him over the years, but this emotional abuse hurt me even more than any belt ever had. At last he finished his tirade, and I fled to my room and sobbed uncontrollably.

Oh God, I whispered, *I wish I were dead.*

That wasn't the end of the ordeal, though. The next day, my stepmother marched into my school and went straight to the principal's office. She launched into another diatribe, announcing to everyone there that I had come home from school wanting to talk about boys and sex. She demanded to know from my schoolmates, who had been summoned by the principal, what they had done to plant all this in my head. I sat shriveled in my seat as she exploded.

"You're too young to be talking about sex!" she shrieked. "Do your mothers and daddies know you got your mind on sex in school when you should be studying?"

Because I wasn't really allowed to socialize outside of school, my stepmother had no idea that these were good, well-behaved young people. We'd never even remotely had the conversations she accused us of. They all denied her wild accusations, but their protests were no match for her rage.

My stepmother turned directly to the boy I liked, stared into his eyes, and spat through clenched teeth, "If I were you, I wouldn't even want her!" Then she turned back to me, her black eyes blazing in some sort of cold triumph.

I was beyond humiliated. I was confused, wounded. I'd reached out for her affection in the best way I knew how, but all she could offer was an outburst of disgust and anger. She seemed to delight in shaming me.

Outside the principal's office I steadied myself against a wall to keep from crashing to the ground, and once again begged God to please strike me down.

•••

HAVING TO DEAL with my stepmother's abuse in the wake of losing my mother was bad enough, but it was exacerbated by not having a father to turn to for any kind of comfort, either. Yes, he was still in the home, but he had never shown much interest in his children, even when Momma was alive.

Short in stature and short in temper, he rarely ever spoke to us, and then only to complain or criticize, like his accusing me of having an inappropriate interest in sex. I don't ever recall him speaking tenderly to us, or telling us that he loved us. His most frequent words to us, usually when he was walking out the door, were a dismissive, "I should have been out fishing when I was making you babies!"

I have no memory of a single real conversation with my father, no hint of tenderness. His philosophy was that children should be seen and not heard. My siblings and I all grew up in fear of him, for it was not uncommon for us to be whipped if he felt we were out of line in any way, no matter how small. He would use his belt or send us out into the yard to get a switch. We learned not to come back with a small one in the hope of escaping a serious beating, because he would just send us out to get a bigger one. If we did try that, he sometimes took the replacement we had and wove it together with the first switch to make an even stronger one.

Corporal punishment wasn't uncommon in those days, but this wasn't about a concerned parent's discipline or correction; this was to inflict pain, plain and simple. He seemed to enjoy it, somehow.

Violence was certainly in his blood. He would beat my mother for no apparent reason, especially when he had been drinking heavily. One afternoon Momma was on the back porch washing clothes, rolling them through a manual wringer to get as much of the water out as possible before hanging them on the line to dry, when he arrived home from work in a particularly foul mood.

I watched, horrified, as he began to slap and push her against the wall. I could not understand where this anger came from. When his rage was spent, my mother quietly went to her bedroom, refreshed her makeup, tidied her hair and clothes, and went back to what she had been doing, as if nothing had happened—just an ordinary day in the life of a coal miner's wife.

My father's lack of concern for his children might be seen to be evidenced in his hasty marriage to my stepmother just a few weeks after our mother's death. He offered no comfort as we grieved, nor did he think to try to prepare us for the arrival of a stepmother, or how confusing that must be to grieving children.

This may not have been just the result of a lack of sensitivity, but because of something more sinister.

My memories of Momma's death are vague, in some ways comfortingly so. I know that it was at New Year, and that she had spent a long time in the kitchen preparing a special traditional meal—collard greens, hog jowls, and black eyed peas to bring prosperity and good luck. With everything ready, she sent us kids off to bed and retired to her own bedroom for some much-needed rest.

Later that night, Daddy shook my older sisters from sleep to tell them that Momma had been taken violently, unexpectedly sick and that he needed to get her to hospital right away. We could hear her gasping in loud breaths. Together with a neighbor's husband, Daddy drove her away. Several hours later he returned home alone and announced that our mother had died.

What happened after that is a blur to me, but my older sisters would tell me years later that, the next morning, they saw my father furtively flushing some pills down the toilet. There was no autopsy, so we'll never know what killed my mother so unexpectedly at just thirty-two years of age.

Wearing a new white dress, a rare purchase made especially for the occasion, I saw snow for the first time the day I watched Momma's casket being lowered into the frosty earth. It was one of the coldest days of my life. As I stood at her graveside amid the tumbling flakes, falling down around me so softly and quietly, I thought it must be God's way of welcoming her to heaven.

I wore the same dress several weeks later when Daddy and our new stepmother were married.

• • •

BETWEEN DADDY'S DISPLEASURE and my stepmother's spitefulness, I cried myself to sleep most nights, longing for some tenderness and care. During my waking hours I learned to be constantly on the alert, careful to avoid doing anything that might set one of them off. Always walking around on tiptoes like that is exhausting to a young heart, crushing the spirit. When fear continues unabated it is corrosive, like an acid eating away inside.

Only later did I realize the toll those years had taken on me. I am not comparing what I went through to the terrible things some of our military servicemen and women have experienced, yet when I read about how the trauma has affected them, I feel like I can identify to some extent.

They say that time is a healer, but I am not so sure. Not in and of itself, at least. Surely, the passage of time provides opportunities for healing, but they have to be taken, and even sometimes pursued. We all know people who have allowed bad things simply to make them bitter as the years go by, not better.

That is what comes to mind as I look back on my neglected childhood.

I don't for a moment diminish the wrongs committed by my father and my stepmother, either deliberately or by default. But I do sometimes wonder what may have happened in their earlier lives to make them so mean, so lacking in even simple care and concern. It may not quite be sympathy, but it's a small sense of sadness for them. I know little about either of my parents' or my stepmother's early lives, other than that Daddy was raised by a relative, not his parents. I don't know the reason, but the absence of a mother and father must have had an impact.

Additionally, life in the South was not easy for anyone when I was small. Slavery may have been abolished in Alabama at the end of the Civil War, but the Northern victory had not marked the end of indentured servitude in my home state. For several decades thereafter, many men convicted of minor crimes, like vagrancy or loitering, were imprisoned and leased by state prisons to private coal mining companies. Nine out of ten of those leased prisoners—slaves by any way of looking at it—were Black. In the early 1900s, nearly ten percent of Alabama's state revenues came from the labor of prisoners leased to private coal companies.

My father, John H. Carbin, went to work at Mulga Mine as a free man, but there weren't a lot of other choices in a small town for someone with only an eighth-grade education. He worked as a shuttle car operator for the Birmingham Coal and Iron Company mine just across the road from our three-bedroom home. His job took him below ground to ensure the smooth passage of the trucks carrying the coal that had been dug from the face.

It was dangerous work. During the life of the mine there were at least three major explosions that claimed a total of almost one hundred lives. A contemporary newspaper account of an explosion in October 1937 said that the blast had been heard in Birmingham, twelve miles away.

Daddy never suffered a serious work accident, but the demanding physical work and exposure to the dusty air took its toll on his body. And his spirit. He came home exhausted and filthy, stripping off his work clothes outside the house to try to keep the soot from getting inside.

It was my thankless job to wash his blackened clothes—though the hardest scrubbing could never get rid of all the smeary residue—and wipe away the black film that inevitably crept inside our home and covered things.

When he came back from the mine mid-afternoon, having started work before dawn, we knew better than to disturb him as he sat quietly in his chair. We would move around carefully, like we were making our way through a minefield, to make sure that we did not upset him.

Not only was the work tough, it was also poorly paid. In forty years as a miner, he never earned more than twenty thousand dollars in a year. So with several children to provide for there was never much money to spare—although he could always find the price of a drink or two.

Through the years, the United Mine Workers to which my father belonged negotiated some improvements in pay and conditions through collective bargaining agreements that typically ran for about four years. These afforded some measure of stability while they were in force, but it was always a difficult season when work stopped as a new contract was negotiated.

With no money coming in and no savings to fall back on, bills began to pile up, and my father was more like a powder keg than ever. The smallest thing could set him off. My siblings and I knew to avoid being in his presence from the time the old contract ended until a new one was agreed upon.

Nor was life easy for my stepmother, or indeed any woman in the poor working South, back then. Though never married, she'd had three children by three different men before marrying my father. That wasn't uncommon, because the men would often go away to work at another mine, or on the railroads, making relationships fluid.

As a result, Momma's experience was something of a contrast. Raised by a stepmother who had mistreated her, Vera Mae Curley left home and married at the age of sixteen. That marriage ended in divorce after a couple of years, leaving her to raise a baby daughter alone until she married my father two years later.

While the coal my father helped mine powered homes throughout the Southeast, that did not include ours. We had no electricity, but we did use coal for the kitchen stove that had to heat the whole house—not that it was particularly large. There was no indoor bathroom; our toilet was an outhouse in the backyard. Water was a precious commodity, and we were allowed a single bath each week—Saturday nights, in a tin tub filled with water heated on the range.

Food was plain and simple, with grits a staple not because it was everyone's favorite but because it was cheap and plentiful. Having been sent to school without any breakfast, by the time lunch came around, our unchanging daily offering—one slice of bologna between two pieces of bread with sandwich spread (a combination of mayonnaise and pickled relish) and a jelly sandwich—seemed like a feast.

Given the financial hardships, we couldn't count on all the basics, much less luxuries. So there were never any feasts or celebrations. Birthdays and Christmases passed without any real acknowledgment, other than for one December when Momma was still alive, and I remember my sisters and I getting Barbie-style dolls to play with; such a rare and unexpected treat.

Despite our modest living conditions, we didn't know that we were poor. All of our neighbors in this small community of less than one thousand people in the segregated South seemed to be in the same situation as my family, eking out an existence as best they could. We were just like everyone else, except in one way.

Because I always had housework to do, and because Daddy did not let us socialize anyway, I did not get to hang out much with other children in the neighborhood. But from the limited interaction I had with them at school, I could tell that, even though their home lives were by no means perfect, they enjoyed some sort of care and comfort, some sense of being loved and cherished, that I and my siblings did not know.

For many years, that hunger gnawed at me more than not always having enough to eat. Parents may not always be able to fill their children's plates, through no fault of their own, but there should never be a reason that they can't fill their children's hearts.

CHAPTER TWO

WHEN I LOOK at one of the few photographs I have of my mother, it's like waking up from a sweet dream that drifts away from you. There is a sense of joy, a longing to go back, to capture what is close but somehow beyond reach. You can't quite remember all the details, but you just know it was good.

In her face I see a playfulness and a firmness. There is the hint of a smile and a sense of resoluteness. She seems to know who she is, and you get a sense that in her considered gaze she knows who you are, too. I get an impression of her kindness and strength of character. There are flowers in her hair, maybe there for some special event, telling me she liked to celebrate. Not that there would have been much opportunity to do so, given her circumstances.

With six children to care for and little money to do it with, Momma didn't have a lot of time or resources to devote to herself. But she always made a point of fixing her makeup and ensuring she looked presentable each morning, offering her brightest and bravest face to the world. Sometimes that would involve disguising the marks left by my father's hands.

I have just snatches of memory. How she would cook us a hearty breakfast before school. The time she would spend combing my hair, her hands firm and gentle on my head at the same time. I also remember her laugh, light and bright. I have no idea what sparked this response, but that she managed to find humor in her hard life speaks to me of her big heart, and how she must have looked for the good in every person and every moment.

Daddy may have been cold, but Momma made home as warm and caring as she could. Though we were still far from affluent, things took a turn for the better when we moved from Mulga a couple of years before she died.

Our new home was in another Birmingham sub-urb, Roosevelt—later to become part of the city of Birmingham—in the promisingly named Village Creek housing development. We lived on Country Club Drive, though the name was more aspiration than in-formation. There was no swimming pool, golf course, tennis courts, or fancy clubhouse. Nevertheless, the three-bedroom, 854-square-foot rambler with a small indoor bathroom, gas heat, and a kitchen with a gas stove was a big step up from our primitive previous situation.

Even so, with a large family we were still packed in like sardines. My older sisters and younger brothers and I all squeezed into a single small bedroom. John and Frankie shared a twin bed, while Barbara, Emma, Sarah and I occupied the full-sized bed—two of us with our heads at the top and two with our heads at the feet.

If Momma was the glue that held us all together, then we started falling apart pretty soon after her death. Indeed, Barbara left home the day of the funeral.

We had not been especially close, not because we were only half-sisters, but because I was timid and shy and she was that much older. In addition, she kept a low profile in the house because of Daddy. If he didn't really tolerate his own children, he had even less time for a child that wasn't his.

All I knew was that some relatives from Momma's side of the family came down from the Detroit area for the funeral, and Barbara went back with them that same day. It would be years before we had any further contact.

Every family is unique in the way its members interact and relate. Remove one, and those that remain have to adjust to new roles and relationships. That is hard enough in healthy homes, and even more difficult when they are dysfunctional. Barbara's departure left

Emma as the oldest child, a responsibility she took seriously. Four years my senior, she tried in some ways to replace Momma, giving us the hugs we needed and making an effort to encourage us. Her nurturing spirit and sensitivity made her especially vulnerable to Daddy's unkindness, but she stayed as long as she could to try to protect the rest of us.

Two years older than me, Sarah was more of a play-mate than Emma because we were closer in age and shared the bond of being left-handed. Though we were the closest, we were also quite different. While I was timid and rule-following, Sarah was the most feisty of all of us; she would stand up for herself against Daddy and my stepmother, only provoking further mistreat-ment from them. One time, when she defied him in some way, Daddy angrily warned her, "I will fight you like you are a man!"

As a result of their clashes, Sarah left home more than once when she was still in school. First she went to live with some relatives in Kentucky for a period, even taking our younger brother John with her. An aunt and uncle from Detroit came to Kentucky to take him back to to live with them. I never saw him again. He stayed in Detroit, while Sarah returned to Alabama for a season. But there was conflict again, so she went and stayed with another family in the Roosevelt area. Sarah got a job and was working and going to school. Her name was listed in the local newspaper as an honor student. That brought attention to Daddy and he was embarrassed that she wasn't living at home, so he decided that she needed to come back.

When Sarah refused, Daddy and our stepmother somehow managed to get her sent to a reform school. There was a court hearing, at which the judge ruled in Sarah's favor. He emancipated her, securing a temporary home with a family while she finished her last few months of high school. On graduation, she left for Detroit.

Emma had remained as the buffer in our home as long as she could. Eventually, when I was thirteen, she could take no more, her flight triggered by an especially ugly episode. For reasons that I can no longer recall but which were probably petty—they usually were— one day my father grabbed her harshly by the arm and ordered her to strip down to her bra and panties. Then he proceeded to beat her mercilessly with his belt, until bright red welts rose all over her skin.

A week later, the signs of that brutal whipping were still evident, the hardened welts abundant and fierce. Emma had lost weight, too, clearly depressed and frightened by this incident. She had stayed as long as she could to try to keep me and my younger brother safe, but now it was obvious that she couldn't even protect herself. She had no choice but to flee, leaving just me and Frankie in the eye of the storm. The scars were so bad on Emma that, to this day, more than fifty years later, she still will not wear a dress above her ankles.

Perhaps because he was that much younger, or due to the fact that he was a boy, Frankie seemed to escape Daddy's displeasure and our stepmother's oppression. That seemed to be reserved exclusively for me. Having been "abandoned" by my sisters, as he put it, Daddy doubled-down on me with his firm, cold hand.

Part of it may have been his anger at the others' departures. While I am sure he was relieved that it meant he had fewer mouths to feed, he likely also felt their leaving held him up in a poor light, so he took out his frustration on me, and made extra-sure I didn't try to challenge his authority.

• • •

SHYNESS AND SHAME can be a crippling combination. As a naturally introverted child with little contact with others outside our home, I didn't have much confidence to begin with. And whatever small amount there may have been was crushed by the continual belittling by my stepmother and my father.

Daddy's silence spoke volumes in its own way, telling me that I wasn't significant enough for him to take notice of or interest in. My stepmother's verbal assaults were usually more direct, telling me that I wasn't good enough and I wasn't going to amount to anything.

Though I never gave her any reason to speak so negatively, always meekly trying my best to do what she and Daddy wanted, my stepmother constantly told me how bad I was. I'd even caught her talking to the neighbors about what a naughty child I was. One time I overheard her telling the woman next door that I had burned the cornbread we were supposed to have for that evening's meal, which was an out and out lie.

No wonder, perhaps, that for a long time I longed to go to reform school or heaven.

Children's hearts are like soft clay; it's easy to make a deep impression on them. If you are told something often enough when you are young without hearing anything to the contrary, chances are you will begin to believe it's true no matter how false it really is. And so I began to wonder if there really was something wrong with me.

One time, weighed down by her barrage of hurtful words, I went to my stepmother and begged her through tears to send me away with all the other bad kids.

"Please," I pleaded. "I want to be good. Let me go to reform school, so I can learn how to be better."

She looked at me with a flash of triumph in her eyes before responding.

"No, child," she said flatly. "That wouldn't do you any good. You're so bad that would just be a waste of time."

With that option dashed, I turned to God and asked Him to simply strike me down instead.

I knew from church that it was a sin to take your own life. People said that suicide would send you straight to hell, and I didn't want that. So I asked God to just let me die, maybe in my sleep.

Although He didn't answer my repeated prayer, I did find comfort in knowing that He was there. Indeed, going to church each week was something of a sanctuary from life at home.

As for many Black, working-class families back in those days, faith was simply a part of life—at least outwardly. How deep those roots went could be open to question, though—Daddy was a church deacon for many years. I don't know how he managed to reconcile the holy man he pretended to be at church with the hard, hateful man he was at home.

However, in small towns throughout the South, the church was not just the center of our spiritual lives, it was also an extended family and helped provide the moral backbone of the community. So there was no question where we would be come Sunday. It was non-negotiable that we'd spend virtually all day in church.

We'd dress up in our finest clothing and head to Friendship Baptist Church, though Daddy attended a local Methodist church, for some reason. I'd start the morning in Sunday School, learning lessons about Jesus. Then I would join Momma for the main service, where she would sometimes sing in the choir. I was part of the junior choir, and when I was old enough

I became a junior nurse, ready to help if anybody got sick. In the afternoons, I was fully focused on the Baptist Training Union, where we were taught more about what it meant to be a good Christian.

It was a day when everything was to be done by the book, and you were expected to comport yourself in a disciplined manner. No short skirts, no daydreaming, and certainly no disrespecting your elders.

• • •

CHURCH WASN'T ALL dry and dull, though. Once a year or so we'd get to attend emotional revival meetings at which people were encouraged to accept Jesus into their lives as their Lord and Savior.

That involved getting up from your pew in response to the preacher's invitation and walking down solemnly to the "mourner's bench" at the front of the church. At the end of the service, a deacon would walk by those sitting there, extend a hand, and ask, "Do you believe?" If they responded affirmatively, they would shake the deacon's hand, and the gesture would signal their welcome to membership. It was not something to be taken lightly.

Something tugged at my heart when I witnessed these moments, but I couldn't bring myself to respond. My stepmother had convinced me that I was too bad, too far gone, for Jesus to really be interested in me.

Yet still I was drawn to Him. Each evening, once all my chores had been completed, I would retreat to a secret spot in my bedroom, hidden behind my bed and next to the wall. I would draw my knees up and read my Bible and pray. I found comfort in the familiar stories.

One night, as I read about the crucifixion of Jesus, it seemed to come to life for me in a new way. I pictured Him alone, without His mother or siblings—just like me—and His friends having fled in terror. I pictured His tormentors stripping the clothing from His back and beating Him brutally until scars rose up upon His back. It reminded me of the many whippings my siblings and I had endured, especially the one that had so wounded Emma in body and spirit. Finally, I pictured Him as He was forced to carry His own cross, the instrument of His demise, to the place of His death.

As a timid child, normally a scene like this would have terrified me. But now, somehow it didn't. Instead, I felt empowered, no longer a helpless little girl but rather an agent of change. Still lying in my hiding place behind the bed, I spoke out clearly and loudly to Jesus.

"I wish I had been there to help You," I told Him.

Something shifted in that moment, as though a tide had turned. The change would not be evident immediately, but I sensed that the direction of my life had begun to turn. With Jesus's help, I was ready to start taking some control of my life.

My first step was to the mourner's bench. At the next revival service, my heart swelled as the preacher spoke about God's love and mercy and forgiveness and invited people to come forward. I got out of my pew and walked up to the front of the church without looking around, though I could feel my stepmother's eyes burning into my back. As I sat on the mourner's bench I felt as though I was being wrapped in a warm blanket of love, like I had finally come home.

When the preacher finished his sermon he came down to where I was sitting, extended his hand, and asked me whether I believed in Christ as my personal savior. I grabbed his hand in return. "Yes," I replied calmly, clearly and forcefully, with no shred of doubt.

Typically, when a young person makes their own profession of faith it's a time of delight for their parents. Indeed, the Bible says that there is rejoicing in heaven when someone comes to salvation, but there was no rejoicing at our home that evening. After the service, my stepmother tried to take all of the wind out of my peace-filled sails.

"It will take more than one revival meeting to wash away all of your sins!" she sneered, her dark eyes a mixture of rage and dismissiveness. Then she ordered me to go back to the mourner's bench at the next revival meeting.

This was borne out of spite, not some misguided sense of spiritual correctness. She just wanted to humiliate me in front of my peers and in the presence of the entire church community, my surrogate family. It was as though she wanted to turn what should have been steps of joy and celebration into a walk of shame. I didn't feel that I could defy her but, embarrassing as it was, I wasn't going to be deterred. If it took ten or twenty or a hundred tries, I was going to keep going back, such was my heart filled with love for Jesus.

So I got up out of my pew and walked forward again at the next revival meeting, not caring what people may have been thinking or whispering. And when my step-mother insisted that I do it again, I did. At the third revival meeting, the preacher once again extended his hand and inquired, "Do you give your life to Christ?" He might have been forgiven for thinking that he hadn't been clear enough when he preached about God's grace being enough to cover anyone and everyone's sin. So my answer was firmer than ever.

"Yes!"

Not only did I have no doubt in my mind, I also realized that I had no more fear of my stepmother, just a sense of love and confidence deep within me. She may have realized that something changed in that moment, or maybe she felt she'd humiliated me enough, but she never said any more about it all.

•••

As I LOOK back on that life passage now, I think of the popular poem "Footprints In the Sand," by Mary Fishback Powers, which describes the last scene of someone's life. Walking with Jesus on the beach, they see only one set of sole marks in the sand behind them.

"Lord, you said once I decided to follow you,

You'd walk with me all the way.

But I noticed that during the saddest and most
   troublesome times of my life,
   there was only one set of footprints.

I don't understand why, when I needed You the
   most, You would leave me."

He whispered, "My precious child, I love you and
   will never leave you,

Never, ever, during your trials and testings.

When you saw only one set of footprints,

It was then that I carried you."

Similarly, I can see God's hand on me, helping me through the storms even if He did not still all the waves and the wind. He gave me the strength to endure, and there were moments that offered me a glimpse of brighter things.

One small source of comfort was Bumpsy, our dog. He had a bad leg after getting hit by a car and being left to recover without any veterinary care. I felt so sorry for him and would spend hours sitting outside in the yard, petting him. He would lean in, giving me rare, warm physical touch in return that I soaked up.

Another bright moment in my dark days came when I was unexpectedly voted high school prom queen in my junior year. Still very introverted and happy to keep to myself, I thought this must be some kind of practical joke, putting the wallflower on display.

My stepmother's actions in confronting my classmates about sex had only further isolated me, making me an unlikely candidate for their selection. Additionally, all the other kids knew we were poor and couldn't afford to attend prom, and they were well aware that I was not allowed out of the house after dark.

Despite those misgivings, I accepted the title with a hope that this might be an opportunity to develop friendships. Indeed, within days of my title being announced, I went from being the little girl stuck in the corner to one of the most popular girls in the class. Everyone was smiling at me, speaking to me, and congratulating me. I was walking on air.

It was simply the best thing that had ever happened to me in my life—until a handsome and popular football player approached me and asked if he could escort me to the prom. It was the first time a boy asked me out on a date.

I didn't know what to say. In fact, at first I wasn't sure that I'd heard him correctly. Gathering my wits, I managed to accept enthusiastically. By the end of the day, the word of my rise in social circles had spread like wildfire, and everyone knew that their new prom queen now had a handsome escort for the prom.

My excitement was clouded by a shadow of concern. Unlike some other girls whose mothers took them shopping regularly, my wardrobe of hand-me-downs from my older sisters and people at church was modest, and I didn't have anything appropriate to wear. On ultra-rare occasions, my stepmother had brought something home for me, but my father had never even taken me shopping, much less paid for anything new. I knew that all I could do was beg him.

I told him about being named prom queen. Expecting a resolute "No," I was shocked when he agreed that I should have a new dress. Maybe he felt he had no choice because everyone knew about my title, or perhaps I caught him in a rare moment of weakness or pity, or maybe guilt.

When we got up early the next morning, I half-expected him to renege on his promise, but we climbed into the car and headed toward downtown Birmingham. His stony silence on the ride could not dampen my spirits; even though he did not say anything, I savored the moment as a rare occasion on which I felt close to my father. I was smiling from ear to ear: Daddy was taking me shopping for a new dress!

When we pulled up outside J.C. Penney, I felt like a million dollars. This was a place I had never visited but had heard the girls at school talk about. It was where the popular, well-dressed kids got their clothes.

The sales assistant in the ladies' department presented us with several options, but none really appealed to me. Then I spotted a dress across the floor that did. As I walked over and took it off the rack and held it up, I knew it was the one. It was a beautiful yellow dress with an empire waist decorated with small beads. Soft pleats cascaded down to the floor like a waterfall. I was certain that it was the most beautiful dress I had ever seen in my entire life.

"And you're in luck," the woman said. "It's on sale."

Despite the reduced price, I still expected Daddy to dismiss it as too expensive. Once again, I was surprised. He didn't protest, but instead got out his wallet to pay $15.99 for the most expensive dress I had ever seen. I felt like I was floating on air as we drove home, despite the familiar silence.

On the morning of the prom, I woke early and finished all of my chores; there was no way I would be allowed out if I did not do all the housework, as usual. By the afternoon, I returned to my room to ready myself, to the best of my abilities, for the evening. I oiled and pressed my hair and gave myself a manicure. I wanted so badly to color my nails, but I did not have any nail polish. Then I put on my new dress. I turned and looked in the mirror and was startled to see such a beautiful girl standing there. In my lovely yellow dress I felt like a burst of radiant sunshine, and looking at myself I cried.

Once I was dressed I heard my father calling. He said that he was ready to drive me to the prom, and my happy bubble burst. I hadn't told him that my date was going to pick me up. In fact, I hadn't told him that I even had a date because I was almost certain that if I did, he wouldn't have allowed me to go to the dance.

There was no way to contact my prom date to let him know that I was going to ride with my father, so I left my room, trembling, and walked into the living room. I had hoped for some acknowledgment of how I looked from Daddy or my stepmother, but there was nothing. Instead, my father simply said, "Okay, let's go." We drove silently to the school, and as he dropped me off, he said he would return at 10:00 p.m. sharp to pick me up. Then he pulled away without a word.

Music and laughter spilled from the gym as I walked in. Festive balloons and streamers hung from the ceiling above my classmates dressed in beautiful gowns and stylish suits. I felt like I had stepped onto the set of a glamorous movie—and I was the star. As I walked in I felt everyone's eyes turning to admire me in my beautiful dress.

Then the magical moment was broken. I saw my prom date who, rather than looking at me with admiration, was glaring at me, clearly upset and angry. He came over and guided me by my arm out of the gym to an isolated spot in the hall. He had gone to my house to pick me up, he said, yelling at me for not waiting for him. I apologized and tried to explain to him that my father had insisted on bringing me to the prom and that I had no way to contact him to let him know. The more I said sorry, the angrier he seemed to get. Finally, he took me by the shoulders and shook me so violently that he tore my new dress. Then he stormed off, not to be seen again that evening. I stood there shell-shocked.

When they announced the class prom queens, I was the only one unescorted to my throne, where I sat alone. But I decided not to let anything spoil this special evening. After the ceremony, there was dancing, food, and punch. I was having a wonderful time, even with the tear in my dress and no escort in sight.

Despite what could have been a major setback when my date left, the time seemed to fly by, and before I knew it 10:00 p.m. had arrived. True to form, my father was waiting in the car when I emerged right on time. And once more, we drove home in silence.

But nothing, not his distance, not my date's disapproval, could rob me of the wonderful feeling of being, even for just a few hours, special.

CHAPTER THREE

WHEN PEOPLE ARE hungry enough they will consume almost anything; it is as though their stomach just needs to be filled with something. I've read of people in North Korea who are so desperate for nourishment that they have eaten grass, like wild animals. Similarly, when someone is starving for love and affection, they can try to fill their hearts with the wrong things. You see it all the time in the problems people have with drugs or alcohol, food or pornography.

I was too young to be drawn into those kind of false comforts as a child, but I did something I am not proud of in an attempt to plug the hole that I had inside from living in a home absent of love and affection. To this day I feel a twinge of embarrassment in sharing about it, even though I know that God's forgiveness covers all our sins, and I have made efforts to "pay forward" for my wrongdoing.

I say "forward" because the Bible explains that God's grace is complete and free—there is nothing we can ever do to repay Him for His gift of salvation. We can seek to be a good example to others, however.

It's not wrong for a child to want to belong, to have a sense of acceptance. In fact, it's an important part of their developing a secure sense of identity. Not finding that at home, I hoped that it might be available at school, but it wasn't so easy. Not only was I introverted by nature, I also stood out to most of the other kids, from my uncared-for appearance and secondhand clothes to my plain-and-simple, same-every-day lunch.

All my classmates wore pretty clothes and shoes, and they had small amounts of pocket change to spend as they wished. Some of them made fun of me and it hurt so badly. I desperately wanted to be like them and decided to take things into my own hands—literally.

From the clothes she wore to the way she carried herself, it was obvious that my classmate Ernestine was loved. One time I was invited to her home where we shared a meal with her family, and I was amazed at how her parents engaged us in conversation and showed interest. I longed for a taste of all that she enjoyed, so when she wasn't looking one day I slipped my hand into her purse and stole some of her money. It wasn't too long before she discovered what had happened and reported the theft to the teacher.

There wasn't quite a trail of crumbs leading from a cookie jar to my seat, but there might as well have been. I'd spent the money on candy and such, and my sudden change of fortune was all too obvious to everyone. I was summoned to the principal's office, where I tearfully confessed what I had done.

Ernestine's unexpected and undeserved kind response gave me the acceptance I'd been looking for all along. She told me that she forgave me, and her generosity of spirit touched me deeply. We even went on to become firm friends for the rest of our time in high school. Though I never saw her again after we left, I still remember her kindness to me when I was confused and alone and looking to belong.

•••

IF I KNEW one thing about the world when I was growing up, it was that it was not a safe place. At home, where I should have been able to enjoy a sense of security, I had to be constantly on my toes. Was Daddy in a particularly bad mood today? What could I do to placate my stepmother? I learned to be as hyper-vigilant behind our front door as I needed to be outside, but for different reasons.

We still have racial problems in the United States today, that is for sure, but things have changed for the better over the past fifty years. It is hard to explain to those who did not grow up Black in the South in the middle of the last century what that experience was like.

One hundred years after the end of the Civil War, the divisions between Black and White ran as deep as ever. Nowhere was that more true than in Birmingham, Alabama, and its surrounding communities. The city is remembered as a focal point of the civil rights movement precisely because that is where change was most needed.

I was never expressly taught about race, but I learned by absorption. The rules of the street were clear. There were two signs posted on public water fountains, lunch counters, and the entrances to department stores. One read "White" and the other "Colored." The potential repercussions for using the wrong facilities were so serious that no one even joked about it.

White citizens had the best of everything, regardless of their economic status or the content of their character. No matter how ill we may be, or how long we'd waited, the doctor would see White patients ahead of us. I remember my mother sitting helplessly in the waiting room with an extremely sick young child, watching forlornly through the glass partition separating the White waiting room from the Colored waiting room, as one White patient after another was kindly ushered in ahead of her. I could sense some of her indignation and humiliation.

Beyond the public signage there was also a long list of unwritten rules. When approaching a White person, anyone of color had to step off the sidewalk to allow the other to pass. Blacks did not initiate conversation with Whites; they only responded when spoken to. Men of color were required to say "Yes, sir" and "No, sir" to young White boys, to avoid a confrontation. Meanwhile, grown Black men were commonly referred to as "boy," another intentional slight.

All of this was just a fact of life that left us walking on eggshells at all times. I remember being ready to run into the house and hide when Whites would come cruising through our neighborhood. One time I actually ducked into the bushes and hid when a rumor swirled that members of the Ku Klux Klan were in the area. It turned out to be bogus, but the fear was palpable. While there were no actual incidences of white-robed Klansmen marching and burning crosses on our lawns, as they did in other places, there was a general air of anxiety.

From time to time a mini-convoy of vehicles would roll down the street with three or four regularly-dressed White men in each vehicle. Sometimes they were armed. They would look out of the windows silently and menacingly, staring as if to say, *We're watching you. Just be careful.* The threat of violence hung heavily in the air. If you happened to be out when such a drive-by occurred, you had to be careful to avoid eye contact; just keep your head down and walk on.

It wasn't uncommon to hear reports of a young Black man being abducted and beaten up, even killed, in more rural parts of the state. In fact, Alabama would go on to have the dubious distinction of being the location of the last known lynching in America, when two young White men murdered Michael Donald in Mobile, in 1981.

When such incidents occurred, there would be no repercussions, no arrests. We learned not to expect protection, and to do whatever we needed to, safety-wise. Many families would black out the windows of their homes at night, so that the light did not leak through and give a drive-by shooter something to aim at.

Our general level of anxiety was heightened following the terrible events of September 15, 1963, when four girls died in the bombing of 16th Street Baptist Church in Birmingham. This brought the ugliness of racism even closer to home—not only was the attack just a dozen or so miles away, but one of the victims, eleven-year-old Carol Denise McNair, was just six months older than me.

News of the awful attack just before the Sunday morning service sent shock waves through the Black community. If we were not safe in God's house, where would we be? People stayed closer to home than usual in the days that followed, fearing there may be some other kind of incident. If they did have to be out and about, they certainly made sure to be home by nightfall.

There was a similar reaction a few years later, when Dr. Martin Luther King Jr. was shot dead as he stepped onto the balcony at the Lorraine Motel in Memphis, Tennessee, on April 4, 1968. Again, it felt like a message was being sent to everyone in the Black community. If someone as well-known and respected as Dr. King was not safe, what hope was there for the nameless rest of us?

It is hard to emphasize enough how deeply the sense of fear sparked by these kind of events ran in Black blood, though Americans of all color got to experience something of a similar dread following the terrorist attacks of September 11, 2001, when for a time, everyone was braced for another horror.

However much of what was happening out in the world made me fearful or uncertain, there was no reassurance offered at home. Daddy remained silent as the struggle for civil rights played out on our black-and-white television. He stayed in his quiet bubble, essentially refusing to even discuss race relations and life as we knew it. I can only speculate as to the reasons; maybe he did not believe that the marches and demonstrations would change things.

Even at the mine, where you might expect shared hardship to bring men together in solidarity despite the differences in the color of their skin, there was ongoing widespread discrimination. Inequality was all my father had ever known, and sadly he might have assumed it would more or less stay that way forever.

With much of the civil rights activity occurring in our home state, I studied the broadcasts carefully. While no one in our house ever went to a demonstration of any kind, I knew that our neighbors could be among those we watched being attacked by dogs and policemen with fire hoses for no other reason than that they wanted to be treated equally. Alarm at the way these activists were treated mixed with a swelling sense of pride.

As I followed these events, I wanted to believe that change was coming, but it all seemed so distant a hope. After all, public schools had officially been desegregated almost a decade earlier by the US Supreme Court's ruling in *Brown v. Board of Education*. But in actuality that had made no difference in our part of Alabama.

The schools I attended were all Black. Continuing inequalities in housing and "White flight" ensured that our schools remained de facto segregated. That meant we got the short end of the stick when it came to resources, an imbalance that was obvious from the roadside. When you drove past the White schools, you would see a well-maintained sports field with spacious and comfortable bleachers. Our less-tended athletics area was surrounded by rickety folding chairs. I once heard someone tell that the White school's science lab had twenty bunsen burners in it, compared to our three.

All this isn't just my potentially biased memory. I recently read an article about a White teacher's memories of Birmingham during those days. He recalled passing a Black school every day where there was a gravel playground and the children walked outside to get to different classes or the restroom. Meanwhile, the White school not far away was a modern brick building with lots of playground equipment, and sports facilities.

A long overdue court ruling in 1970 finally ordered the integration of my high school. We arrived on the day to be met at the school doors by police officers with dogs, water hoses, guns, and clubs. Many of them seemed to be just waiting for someone to step out of line and give them an excuse to let loose. But any such hopes were dashed, because no White students turned up; their parents simply refused to send them.

This was sad, if not entirely surprising, but in other parts of Alabama attempts to equalize opportunities in education turned out to be almost laughable. When they tried to enforce integration in one county, the move backfired. The idea had been to increase the number of White teachers at Black schools, but it turned out that some of those already working there didn't have the degrees that were required.

Because of a quiet system of unspoken prejudice, while Black teachers had to have graduated to get a post, some of their White equivalents had been hired without having done so, being allowed to study for their qualification during their vacations. As a result, the attempt to rebalance the teaching mix by redistributing what had to be qualified staff ended with many of the White teachers who were there needing to be replaced by qualified Black teachers from other counties.

•••

ALTHOUGH I GREW up with a general suspicion, if not outright fear, of White people, I did not encounter many directly as a child. There were a couple of White teachers at the Black schools I attended, but I did not have much contact with them, and other than that my small world—home, school, church—was all African American. My first meaningful interaction with a White person came when I left high school, and it only confirmed any stereotypes I may have held.

As a disciplined student who always conscientiously did what was required, I was an above-average student at school, always bringing home As and Bs, but I had never really stood out. By nature I was reserved, and always having to be home right after the last bell to do housework meant that I never took part in any extra-curricular activities. I mostly flew under the radar: I doubt whether any of the teachers would remember me, though I can recall one middle school teacher, in particular, who encouraged my love of math, which would prove significant. When it came time for me to leave Roosevelt High, I had no thoughts of a life being possible beyond Mulga.

There had been occasions when I had contemplated my sisters' example and considered leaving, but only momentarily. Where could I possibly go, and whatever would I do? I felt a responsibility to stay for Frankie, and for some reason I also accepted that it was my duty to help look after my two younger half-siblings, Timothy and Felicia. From the time they were born, I had babysat and cared for them. Additionally, as a more passive kind of person than my sisters, I believed in following the rules, even if my father's were unreasonable. And I had been so beaten down by my stepmother's constant hammering that I would never amount to anything that I accepted her verdict as reality.

So on leaving high school, I ended up taking a job at a small diner in downtown Birmingham. The clientele was White, as were most of the staff. The few Black girls employed there were bus girls. Only White women got to be waitresses—not only earning a higher hourly wage but also getting all the tips. We Black girls were like ghosts, slipping in after the customers left their tables to clean up. It was as though we didn't exist.

In what I would learn was a fairly common form of quiet prejudice, the owner never outright said Whites were better than Blacks but he took every subtle and sometimes not-so-subtle opportunity he could to make it clear that's what he believed. He seemed to delight in putting a Black person in their place, never missing an opportunity to denigrate or belittle one of us for some small infraction. As a Black employee you could never do anything quite right.

He even decided, like some latter-day slave owner, that he could change our names. He repeatedly called me Julie. I don't know where it came from, but one day I summoned up the nerve to tell him that, no, my name was Juliette. It made no difference.

Much as I needed the money, I could see that working here offered no future. There was nothing to look forward to, just day after day in a dead-end job and then home to more chores where I didn't even get to earn some small income. My stepmother and my father still expected me to do all the things I'd had to while I was at school: clean the bathrooms, do housework, wash the clothes. Now I was more like an unpaid, live-in maid. I yearned for something more, but just didn't know where to turn. Church on Sunday was my only bright spot, a brief reprieve from the drudgery of my other days. Something simply had to change.

The opportunity came through Carzell, the youngest of my three stepbrothers. Though he and his brothers didn't move in with us when their mother came, we saw them from time to time. I resented having to do their laundry, along with everyone else's, but I didn't have anything against them personally, and I became quite close to Carzell. His mother's favorite, he was just a couple of years younger than me, so we spent some time together. He had striking features and a warm personality that was in such contrast to his sharp, cold mother.

While I was working at the restaurant, Carzell graduated from high school and enrolled at Alabama State University, a public historically Black school a couple of hours' drive away in Montgomery. He was the first from his family to go to school, and my stepmother worked with the school to get him a full ride.

One day, it dawned on me: if there was life beyond his home on Letson Street in Woodward for Carzell, why not me too? Up until this point, while I had known that I could leave home whenever I wanted, I had felt trapped by my lack of opportunities. But Carzell's example was like a flicker of light in my darkness.

Without telling anyone, I contacted Alabama State. When a few weeks later I received a letter telling me I had been accepted, I was so excited that I simply burst into tears. I felt like I had been given a key that could unlock the door of the prison I had been in for so long. I read and reread the letter countless times to reassure myself that I had not gotten it wrong. Nope, there it was: I was accepted for the fall semester, just three months away.

Now a flood of questions rolled in. How on earth would I ever pay for school? Was I really bright enough to handle it? I would be arriving there older than most of the other freshmen; would they accept me?

Was I really ready for this, or was it just a crazy way of trying to get away from home? And perhaps most importantly of all: How on earth could I tell Daddy and my stepmother what I had in mind?

With so many thoughts rushing through my head, it took me a couple of days to work up the courage to tell them. Taking a deep breath and saying a quick prayer asking for God's help, I finally went into the living room and found them sitting in their usual places, my father in his recliner and my stepmother in her overstuffed La-Z-Boy. They both looked directly at me as if they knew I had something to share.

My head turned from one to the other as I opened my mouth, but no words would come out. Then I raised the letter in my right hand.

"I got in," I said. "Alabama State has accepted me." I went on in a rush, to try to head off any objection they may raise. I explained that it wasn't going to cost them anything—I would pay my own way, somehow.

Having delivered my exciting news, I stood and waited. Despite a lifetime of indifference, I still hoped for something, some token of affirmation or encouragement. I wanted Daddy to tell me well done, and that he was proud of me.

He didn't say anything for what felt like the longest time, just looking at me with the same blank stare he always gave me. Then he spoke.

"When are you leaving?"

CHAPTER FOUR

O THER THAN THE first time I walked down to the mourner's bench and gave my heart to Christ, there is no single more important day in my life than bright, sunshiny September 22, 1972.

That is because the many wonderful things I have experienced since, the birthdays and anniversaries and special moments I have been privileged to enjoy, all resulted from my arrival at Alabama State University.

I stood on the sidewalk with all my worldly possessions in a small suitcase and two garbage bags as my father pulled away from the curb and drove home without a word or a backward glance.

The journey there from Brighton in our family's Deuce and a Quarter had been silent, naturally. There were no words of encouragement or affirmation, no wishing me well. If anything, Daddy seemed annoyed to have to make the ninety-minute trip. But nothing could dampen the sense of anticipation inside me as we drove.

Other than for one day trip to Chattanooga to see relatives, I had never traveled beyond Birmingham; as unfamiliar scenery rolled by, I felt like I was heading into a foreign country.

Daddy broke the silence with a curt, "We're here," as he pulled up outside Abercrombie Hall. I got out and stood in awe of the elegant, red-brick residence. Then my reverie was broken by the sound of a car door slamming.

Turning around, I saw that my father had taken my things out of the trunk, placed them on the ground, and gotten back into the vehicle.

"I'm going to head back because I have some things to take care of at home," he said. Not even waiting to check that I was in the right place, he drove off without a wave, leaving me to find my own way once again.

Neither Daddy's coldness nor the heat of the day as I picked up all my things could reduce the excitement I felt. For the first time in my life, I had a sense of anticipation. A door had opened into a whole new world, and I was ready to step through it and explore.

Reaching the entrance to my new home, I went inside and found the stairs that would take me to my room on the third floor.

"It looks like you could do with some help."

The voice from behind me was warm and bright. I turned around to see a smiling girl of about my age walking toward me. She reached for the two trash bags clasped in my left hand, and asked, "What floor are you going to?"

We paused to catch our breath when we got to the third level. My friendly helper told me that she lived up on that floor too, and asked me my room number. I couldn't remember, so I reached into my purse to pull out a piece of paper with the details on it. The girl saw it and shrieked, "Oh my God! That's my room! You're my roommate!"

And that's how I came to meet Vivian, who would not only prove to be a great help to me as I adjusted to college life, but would become a forever friend.

Room 223, at the rear of the building and overlooking a small garden, wasn't large. In it were squeezed two beds, two dressers, two small tables, and two small closets. But for someone who had spent much of her life sharing a room with five others, it felt like a penthouse suite. Though it was basically furnished, I was convinced that it was the nicest dorm room in the world. Not that I had seen one other than in a school brochure before.

I had arrived at Alabama State sight unseen. Usually, students visit at least some of the schools they have in mind to attend, to help them make their final decision. I had applied only to Alabama State and never considered a visit, in part because I did not want my father to know what I was considering. I feared that if he learned I was planning to leave home, he might try to prevent it somehow.

I had, however, enlisted my stepmother's help. Knowing that she had managed to somehow secure all of Carzell's funding for his time at school, I asked her to help me with my application for financial help. That I would risk being dismissed, as happened so typically whenever I asked my stepmother for anything, was a sign of just how desperate I was to see a change in my circumstances.

To this day I don't know what prompted her to help. Did she feel guilty for all of her mistreatments, maybe? Had she decided that, much as she liked having me around as a sort of live-in maid, she actually more wanted me out of the house? Whatever motivated her, I am grateful for the help she gave in securing some financial assistance that made it possible for me to attend.

Beyond the loans I qualified for and the Work Study program for which I had been accepted, the financial resources I arrived with at Alabama State comprised my meager life savings: a grand total of $62.39 accumulated in a jar with a bill here and a few coins there over my two years working at the restaurants.

If I had stopped to think about it all, I might have been overwhelmed by what I had taken on in going to

Alabama State. I arrived with everything I owned and hardly any money, but I wasn't worried about what lay ahead. Somehow, I just knew that everything was going to work out fine.

Having helped me to what turned out to be our room, Vivian waited while I unpacked. Given that I did not have much, it did not take too long. Then she gave me a tour of the campus to help me get acclimated.

It ended in the quad down in front of our dorm, where we sat to people-watch. It was already clear in the small amount of time we had spent together that I was the quiet partner in this new duo, while Vivian was the more outgoing one. I was content with this arrangement; so much was new to me that it was quite overwhelming.

As we sat, Carzell came by. He knew that I was arriving on campus that day, and he dropped by to see if I was settling in okay. Normally I would have been happy to see him, but I found it hard to concentrate on all his questions.

My attention was taken up by the inordinately handsome young man who was with him. His roommate, I was told. Even forty years later, I can picture his "bad boy" outfit of bell-bottom pants and a jean jacket with the sleeves cut off. It covered him up, but there was no denying that underneath those layers he possessed a great body. Topping it all off was a big Afro and a mustache. I was smitten.

That attraction was enhanced when James McNeil, as he introduced himself to me, opened his mouth and the most melodious voice emerged. I had never heard an accent like that before in my life; so sultry and exotic it was as if he were from some foreign land.

We had only a brief exchange, but I was captivated by his outgoing personality and his great sense of humor. I immediately knew this was the man of my dreams, and that I wanted to marry him.

I could not get James off my mind for the rest of the evening. Of course, my father and my stepmother would have been horrified to know the thoughts that were coursing through my mind. They had reluctantly allowed me to attend college for an education, not to mess around with boys. But there was no denying that I'd met the most incredible man I'd ever know.

So much had changed in a single day by the time I lay my head down on my pillow that night. Like someone released after a long prison sentence, I felt as though a big load had been taken off my shoulders. Where once I had seen no future, now it seemed there were no limits.

In the space of a few hours, I'd begun a lifetime of opportunity, made a lifetime friend, and discovered a lifetime love.

• • •

JAMES AND I came from backgrounds that were similar and different at the same time. Like me, he had grown up poor—just a couple hundred miles away, in Chatom, southwest Alabama—and lost a parent when he was a child. His father died when he was two. Money was tight as a result, and dinner would often be just cornbread and buttermilk. When he got older, he would supplement the menu with squirrels and rabbits he caught in the woods.

The youngest of four by several years, James mostly grew up alone with his mother, as his older siblings left home one by one. Unlike my father and stepmother, James's mother wanted more for her son, encouraging him in his education and planting the idea that one day he would go to college. Although it was the county seat, Chatom was so small that the local library consisted of just two bookshelves inside the fire station, which James read his way through one summer.

James had arrived at Alabama State on a music scholarship. A talented trumpeter, he had played in a band while in high school to make some money, and won scholarships to three Alabama schools: the University of West Alabama, Troy State, and Alabama State. On his mother's advice, he chose Alabama State for its smaller and almost exclusively Black student body and found himself rooming with another freshman named Carzell.

With similar personalities—lively, warm, and outgoing—they hit it off well, and continued to room together into their second year, when I arrived on campus.

My second day at Alabama State featured the freshman dance, which provided us newcomers with an opportunity to get together and meet our peers. Many upperclassmen often also attended the dance as well, to check out the female freshmen, and it made for a great time.

It was a festive scene in the gymnasium, with all types of punch, snacks, and cookies. Most everyone was on the dance floor as the DJ spun the latest tunes...except for Vivian and me. As, apparently, the only people there with two left feet, we stood off to one side and watched, trying not to look like a couple of wallflowers. Just as we were starting to feel desperate, I spotted someone across the crowded room: James McNeil.

Until that moment, I'd spent my life as a classic introvert, eyes usually cast down to avoid making face-to-face contact with anyone, and mostly content with my own company. But something came over me that night; it was as though stepping onto the campus had unlocked possibilities for me.

It seemed like a long way across the gym, but without any kind of hesitation I walked over and said hello. A true gentleman, James was exceptionally polite and asked if I was enjoying myself. We fell into a light, easy conversation.

Things were going well until he asked me to dance. I was mortified; this would mean making a fool of myself. I told him that although I really liked the music, I couldn't dance a step to save my life.

He laughed, in his smooth baritone.

"I'll teach you," he said, taking me by the hand and leading me to the dance floor. Our first couple of moves were very awkward, but he quickly made me feel at ease, and soon we were dancing the night away. Far from home for the first time, I was having the best time of my life.

For someone who hadn't wanted to dance to begin with, I was sad when we finally had to stop when the evening came to a close. James walked me back to my dorm room and kissed me on my cheek, once again a perfect gentleman.

Apart from some puppy-love crushes in high school and the disappointment of my prom night experience, I did not know much when it came to relationships, but I knew one thing without a doubt: I was hopelessly, head-over-heels in love.

The only problem was that the object of my affection did not seem to be quite as interested in me. He had been courteous and charming, but he did not seem to be particularly interested in pursuing me. Indeed, I would learn later that he was casually seeing someone else at that time. Hardly surprising. Given his looks and personality, he was something of a catch.

I was not going to be put off, however. I made excuses to see him every day; dropping by his room on the pretext of wanting to see Carzell, or making sure I was in the right place somewhere else when he turned up.

I didn't have much in my favor. I was a plain Jane, with bad skin and crooked teeth and no curves anywhere. Nor did I have any idea how to do my hair, apply my makeup—though I made an effort to do so every morning, as a matter of routine—or dress in a flattering manner. I had been too young for my mother to offer any coaching before she died, and my stepmother had made it all too clear that I could not turn to her for help in this important area of a young woman's development. I was on my own.

Despite all that I lacked, I was not to be deterred, however. My persistence paid off, and our relationship began to blossom in every way possible. The natural result was that James and I made love for the first time.

I cried afterwards, much to James's consternation, but not in pain or regret. Despite my lack of experience, and the likely objections if anyone at home ever found out about it, I just knew it was right. I'd heard horror stories from other girls about their first times, but mine proved to be joyful. And though I'd always assumed that my first lovemaking would occur on my wedding night—after all, that's how it was "supposed" to be—the timing for my first time was impeccable.

My tears were for joy because James had been so gentle and tender, and everything about that night made me feel special. After explaining that to him, he relaxed, and we spent the rest of the night lying in each other's arms.

• • •

FALLING IN LOVE had not been in my plans when I arrived at Alabama State. While meeting James left me feeling like I was dancing on air, I knew that I still needed to keep my feet on the ground. School was my gateway to a new life, and while that unexpectedly seemed to include James, I could not afford to waste the opportunity I had been given.

So I threw myself into my studies, making sure that I was attentive in every class, always diligent in completing assignments. In addition, I had my Work Study duties to attend to. I was given a job in the snack bar, which I really enjoyed. I was used to hard work, so that wasn't a problem. In fact the fifteen hours a week I had to complete were considerably less than the time it took to do all my weekly chores at home. And it was refreshing to have people say please and thank you rather than ignore me. For an introvert, it was also a great way of getting to interact with other people.

Some of the other students complained about things—whether it was the classes or the faculty or the facilities—but I couldn't understand their grumbling. I was just so happy to be there, enjoying life under a bright, open sky after so many years of being locked up and boxed in.

In fact, this new freedom was so important to me that I couldn't face the prospect of losing it, even for a moment: I never went home during my entire college stay.

One reason for that was because I wanted to graduate in three years rather than the usual four—partly to reduce my costs and partly because, having arrived a couple of years behind my peers, I felt that I had some catching up to do. As a result, I stayed on at Alabama State for summer school and remained there for other holidays; there were a number of students who could not go home for one reason or another, so the snack bar was still busy.

Although between my class work and snack bar work I was quite busy—not to mention my growing relationship with James—I found time to enjoy some of the wider experiences of college life. Among them was joining a sorority. With its emphasis on social service projects and no financially demanding campus residence, Zeta Phi Beta was an ideal fit for an introvert with no money. I made some new friends through our community projects and social events.

Bit by bit, my confidence was being established. Doing well in school and developing relationships with people who affirmed and accepted me for who I was helped blow away the smog of hopelessness that had hung over me for so long. One measure of that change was when I ran for and was chosen to be the school's Miss Hornet. My responsibilities included riding in the annual Thanksgiving Parade and appearing at sporting and other events. This fun season helped soothe another bruise from my past, replacing any lingering hurt from my high school prom queen experience— wondering whether I'd been selected as a joke or out of pity, and hurt by my date's mistreatment—with a sense of belonging.

Having completed general classes in my freshman year, I had to choose a major as I entered my second. I chose Economics. I wasn't sure what I would do with that, maybe teach, but I had always found numbers to be easy. It was something that seemed to run in the family; both Emma and Sarah also had a facility with figures, and would both work with money at some stage. In my case, I wonder whether the draw to numbers was in part because, unlike people, they were dependable and uncomplicated, in that what you saw is what you got. You didn't have to try to find any hidden meanings. Handled carefully, they always added up! Then there was my attention to detail, which had been fine-tuned by years of having to do things around the house just so or get told off and made to do it again. I had learned to take my time and be precise.

After several classes and consultations with my adviser and my accounting professor, they informed me that a major in Accounting would afford me more job opportunities than an Economics degree. I took heed of their advice and quickly changed my major to

Accounting, which would prove to be a pivotal decision. Participating in Alabama State's co-operative education program, which combined classroom studies with work placements, gave me a taste for what accounting involved in the real world, and I fell in love with it.

In addition to my academic leaning, my appreciation of accounting as a worthwhile career was heightened by my own personal awareness of the importance of money—especially when I had very little. Even with my scholarships and work study income, I had to be very frugal. I tried not to feel jealous when girlfriends excitedly opened letters from home with gifts of a couple of hundred dollars inside.

Though I had been determined to make it on my own, there were a couple of occasions when my financial situation was so tight that I wrote home, asking Daddy if he could help in any way. One time I received an envelope from home containing two dollars.

Seeing how my co-operative education placement was helping me, James decided to do the same thing, a decision that would set him on a new course. Having arrived at Alabama State on a music scholarship, he soon recognized that a good ear and a natural talent were not going to be enough; he would need to learn to read music and apply himself more. That realization prompted him to switch majors to Political Science and History, with the idea of maybe becoming a lawyer.

Meanwhile, his co-operative placement took him for a semester to the Naval Construction Battalion Center in Gulfport, Mississippi, home to the famous Seabees. During his time there, his supervisor took a shine to him and did all that he could to give James a positive experience. He met with him personally to share his wisdom and experience, and made sure that he got to rotate through all the different departments to get a broad overview of the operations. At the end of his three-month placement, James returned to Alabama State with a new awareness of and interest in the opportunities available through some sort of government service.

If anything, James's school circumstances were even more difficult than mine. All he had brought to Alabama State from home had been two plates and a quilt. To meet his school costs he had to work two jobs while juggling classes. He would work more than fifty hours a week, evenings at a department store and then nights at the UPS center. Daytime was for classes, with naps whenever he could snatch them.

James's mother may not have been able to serve up elaborate meals when he was young, but she had made sure to feed his soul. She was generous with physical affection and encouraging words. "Remember who you are," she would tell him repeatedly. "You're James McNeil." Her message was that while they may not have much, that didn't matter. He was still special. He still mattered. The message that he was somebody—in marked contrast to the one I had grown up hearing, that I was nobody—gave him a quiet confidence and determination that was attractive.

Along with his courtesy, good looks, and the way he gave me his attention, signaling that I mattered and what I had to say mattered—a far cry from what I had experienced—his personality opened doors for him, including to my heart. Not all of my friends were as positive, however; they felt that maybe he didn't come from quite the right stock, and that I could probably do better.

With money in short supply, we didn't go out on many actual "dates," but we enjoyed just spending time together. We would meet for breakfast in the cafeteria, and lunch. We'd sit outside on a wall on the campus, and watch the world go by. Sometimes we might go to downtown Montgomery and wander around together.

Perhaps I should have been more alert when, one evening in my junior year, James took me for dinner at The Filling Station, a fun restaurant in a converted gas station in the Montgomery area. Two old gas pumps outside testified to its former use, but inside, the place had been converted into an elegant dining area. I was awed by the fine white linen tablecloths, the gleaming chandeliers, and the perfect romantic lighting. The all-male army of waiters dressed in tuxedos was so attentive to my every need that it almost made me uncomfortable. I had never been anywhere as fancy in my life.

Once seated, I was floored by the telephone-book-size menus full of exotic-sounding dishes. Fortunately, James picked up on my discomfort and confusion and calmly offered to order for me. I quickly said, "Yes." Despite the initial shock, I soon settled, in and we shared an unbelievable three-course meal. I was thoroughly enjoying this unique experience.

As we finished our dessert, just when I thought the evening was ending, a waiter set down another covered plate in front of me. He deftly removed the lid, and there sat the most beautiful engagement ring that I had ever seen in my life.

James had presented me with a promise ring in our second year together, a token of commitment I had received delightedly. We had not talked much more directly about our future together since then, so this proposal caught me off-guard. The reality was more than I could handle; I felt all my old insecurities rising up. Though I had thought I had shrugged off my hurtful high school prom date experience, it had left a mark: deep within, I felt that if something seemed too good to be true, then it probably was!

"Really?" I asked. "You want me to marry you? I can't imagine why..."

James smiled gently. "Yes, I want you to be my wife."

Somehow, through the tears, I managed a joyfully loud "Yes!" that may have been out of place for the elegant surroundings, but which I was too excited to hold back. No one around us seemed to mind, however; they turned and applauded as we held hands across the table.

We left The Filling Station on cloud nine, and not even the backstory James shared to his proposal could bring me down to earth. Indeed, what he told me just illuminated how wonderfully my life had changed since arriving at Alabama State.

Wanting to do the right thing, James had called my father to ask permission to propose, he told me. Daddy had given a resolute "No!" and even told James that I had said he and I were no longer dating. Estranged as we were, my father was still trying to control my life. Recognizing my father's attempt to thwart our relationship by blatantly lying, James decided that he could not be expected to honor such deceit. Having tried to follow convention, he realized that he needed more to follow his heart.

CHAPTER FIVE

IN SOME WAYS, I look back on my time at Alabama State as like being on Noah's Ark. It was a safe space from the storm, and I found my two-by-two partner there. I began to discover there was some warmth in the world. But the time came to leave the security it offered and venture out into new territory.

I had changed in many ways during my three years on campus. I was still something of an introvert, but I was far more confident in myself. I had discovered that people liked me for who I was. I had learned that I was strong and capable. I had found that there was more kindness than cruelty in the world. After a childhood spent constantly lowering my expectations to meet a lesser reality, I had discovered that life offered more.

As a result, returning to Brighton after graduation seemed like a backward step, but with no job immediately lined up, I had no other real options. Within a day of being back under the same roof as Daddy and my stepmother, I knew that I could not stay. I had breathed fresh air for the past three years, and simply could not survive in that toxic atmosphere any more. Frankie drove me back to Montgomery, where I hoped some sort of opportunity would open up.

I went back to the placement office on campus, where I had previously pursued potential openings without success. One of the staffers was updating the job placement board, and I told her I was looking for an accounting-related opening.

"Today might be your lucky day," she said with a smile, pointing me to a job posting for an entry-level accounting position with the State of Alabama Revenue Department. I immediately walked over to the nearby applicant's room, sat at a vacant desk and called the contact person indicated on the job posting. After a brief conversation, I was asked to come in the next day for an interview, after which I was hired on the spot.

And, so just one week after graduating, I began my accounting career with a job paying an annual salary of $5,500—an unbelievable sum for a coal miner's daughter who had never had more than a few dollars to her name. Once again, I reflected on how the educational opportunity I had been afforded had so radically changed my life.

The job auditing business revenues was exciting for a newly qualified accountant, but it did not last long. I started work there in August and was on the move by the following May. Walking away from a secure position with future prospects was something of a sign of my growing self-confidence, but also a marker in my and James's relationship.

Having taken the more common four years to complete his studies, James had graduated a few months after me, in December, and found work in Harrisburg, Pennsylvania. He had landed a great position thanks to the man who had mentored him while he was in his cooperative education placement. For some reason, the man had decided to keep James on his roll, though he was no longer being paid, when he returned to school. This meant that James chalked up extra-credit time for government service, so when he took the Professional and Career Administrative Exam for prospective government hires, he was one of around fifteen hundred taken in nationwide.

When James came back to collect me in his two-door, limited edition Ford, I was a little nervous. My world had been enlarged during my time at Alabama State, but I still hadn't seen much of it in person. A work experience placement at the Patuxent River Naval Base in Lexington Park, Maryland, while in school, and that one-off family trip to Chattanooga remained the only times I had actually been out of my home state. I didn't know what to expect, but I was curious to see what life was like in the North, and I figured that as long as I was with James, everything would work out.

We drove past Birmingham on the thirteen-hour drive, but I had no interest in visiting my father and stepmother. That was no longer home. Instead it was a freshly painted townhouse in a row of multiple-level homes very different to the one-level, standalone houses I was familiar with. And although each one was a bit different, they were designed to form a cohesive grouping that was very pleasing to the eye.

At first I thought the large building we had parked in front of was all ours, and I was taken aback, but James set me right. He led me round the back to stairs that took us up to the fourth floor. Unlocking the door, he opened it and turned to me.

"Welcome home."

It was by no means grand, but after sharing a small house with a large family for years, and then a college dorm, it felt like a palace. There was a small kitchen with a table and two chairs, with a living room to the right that had a sofa and a chair. Connected to the bedroom was a bathroom with a claw-foot tub; the first I had ever seen. I thought it was so beautiful, like something out of a magazine.

Looking around, I asked James where all the furnishings had come from. Goodwill, he told me, having to explain it was a thrift business when I looked blank. I was startled when he told me he bought everything for just three hundred dollars.

The discoveries continued, revealing just how much I still had to learn. Some people have to overcome a sheltered childhood, in which they may have been overprotected but with good intent. In my case it was more a question of having been shuttered; kept locked away. My horizons may have broadened while I was at Alabama State, but they had been so narrow when I arrived there that I still had a long way to go.

Once we had finishing unloading the car, I asked James what we were going to do about eating.

"Let's go to Mother's," he said.

"What's mother's?"

"It's a sub shop," he told me.

"What's a sub shop?"

And so I had my first-ever Philly cheese steak, washed down with a glass of lemonade.

When I woke up the following morning, I found myself alone. There was a note from James on the nightstand saying that he would see me at 4:00 p.m. There was no food in the apartment, so I headed out to a grocery store I remembered seeing the night before when we went to Mother's.

As I neared the store, a fragrant smell of warm, fresh bread tickled my nose. It was coming from the sub shop, which had just opened. I went in for a breakfast sandwich, selecting a bacon, egg, and cheese sub and a cup of herbal tea. I took a window seat and enjoyed my delicious breakfast, soaking in the simple pleasure.

Suitably fortified, I went to the grocery store to buy the ingredients I would need to surprise James with his favorite meal; cube steak smothered in onion gravy, with rice and biscuits.

By the time James came home, the meal was ready, with a small bouquet of flowers brightening the center of the table. He smiled with delight. We ate and talked for what seemed to be hours, simply enjoying being together. We may not have had much, but we had each other, and that seemed to be more than enough.

While love may make the world go round, it doesn't pay the rent, however, and I knew that I couldn't just play homemaker forever. I'd need to find a job—after the wedding.

• • •

PSALM 68 SAYS that God "sets the lonely in families," and that was our experience as James and I prepared for marriage.

Neither of us thought of inviting any of our relatives to be part of our celebration when we exchanged our vows. There was no way I wanted my father and stepmother to be there, and I'd sadly lost contact with my siblings. James didn't have the same kind of painful memories I did, but had become distanced from his family in his own way. We planned to just do our own thing—until Gladys and Millie got involved.

They were a couple of older women working in the naval office where James was starting out, learning about inventory control. He had charmed them, as he did so many others, and they had sort of adopted him as their shared son. They looked out for him at work and invited him over to their homes for dinner, and along to church, in his early days as a newcomer to Harrisburg who didn't know anyone there. Figuring he was quite a good catch, they even tried to set him up with various nieces and even Gladys's own daughters, until he made it clear he had a fiancée to whom he was committed.

They did not seem too upset by that news, because they soon took me under their wings too. And when they heard we were going to get married without anyone there, they put their feet down. They would host and pay for our wedding, they told us. We were deeply touched. For me, especially, it was so unusual to have people go out of their way to be kind.

With only a couple of months in which to prepare, thankfully the arrangements were minimal. There were no invitations to send out, and Gladys and Millie said they would cater the food for the few guests, some friends from James's work. They also knew the best baker in town from whom to order a small cake.

The wedding was set for Saturday, July 3, 1976, at Italian Lake, a beautiful garden setting in the center of the city, not far from the banks of the Susquehanna River. The day dawned auspiciously, bright and warm, as I began to get ready. Like all the other arrangements, my preparations were less demanding than for many weddings. I did not have a wedding gown to put on just so; with no one to guide me in the process, I had chosen a simple blue dress.

Everything was going well until thirty minutes before the simple ceremony was to begin. Then, out of nowhere, a fierce midsummer storm blew in, with golf-ball-sized hail forcing us to make an eleventh-hour change of plan. Fortunately, our low-key event made that not too stressful. There were no large flower arrangements, no chairs, no trellises or runners that needed to be moved. Nor was there a maid of honor, bridesmaids, flower girls, and groomsmen to reorganize. We just moved the proceedings across the street from Italian Lake to the home of Millie's brother, Cecil, and his wife, Claire.

Home weddings are not entirely uncommon, but they usually take place in rather more grand surroundings. Cecil's home was no antebellum mansion with vaulted ceilings and sweeping stairways, just a cozy little suburban house. But it felt perfect to us, symbolizing how these dear people had literally taken us into their hearts and their homes.

The pastor of Millie's Holiness church performed the ceremony in the small living room, in front of fewer than a dozen guests. James chose not to have a best man, and I, of course, was not given away by my father—which was fitting, because he had never really claimed me in the first place. Instead, I walked forward to James on Cecil's arm.

I had long ago given up on expecting anything from Daddy, so there was no sense of disappointment, no feeling that my wedding day was incomplete. I was just so happy to be committing myself to James for the rest of my life. If there was one small dampener on the day, it was that my mother wasn't there to share in her daughter's happiness. I believe she would have smiled.

Putting some last-minute finishing touches to my makeup upstairs before the ceremony, I could see ice falling from the sky as I looked out of the window. And I could hear James and the minister talking downstairs.

Normally confident and assured, something I loved about him, James sounded a little anxious. He asked the minister whether the bad weather was some kind of an omen; maybe he shouldn't be getting married? I held my breath for a moment.

"Oh no, by no means," I heard the pastor reply. "Most couples only get a few showers of blessings on their big day. You're getting an ice storm of love! That must mean you and Juliette are going to have a long and strong marriage." The two men laughed together.

Letting out a sigh of relief, I finished fixing up and went downstairs. James was waiting there in the first suit he ever bought. Exuding his usual quiet confidence, he had a big smile on his face that gave no hint of the momentary doubt I had eavesdropped on.

Having exchanged our vows, we shared some simple refreshments and cake with our witnesses before leaving for a brief honeymoon—back at our apartment. Not only were we unable to afford to go anywhere exotic, I also had to report to my new job in a couple of days. We left Millie's home in style, however, in the rear of a fancy limousine someone lent us for the day.

I arrived at the regional offices of Blue Cross Blue Shield as the new Mrs. Juliette McNeil, the wedding band still delightfully unfamiliar on my finger. Helping develop insurance rates wasn't my first choice, but it was a good position in a diverse and welcoming environment as we adjusted to married life.

During the three years I was there, James was quickly developing a reputation for his ability in the naval office. He started traveling quite a bit within the US, and weekends would often find us in Washington, DC, or Philadelphia, either related to his work or just for fun. For the most part, life together was wonderful, though like all couples we did our share of learning about each others' preferences and idiosyncrasies.

The biggest single bump we hit came on our first wedding anniversary. Having become accustomed to and appreciative of James's thoughtfulness and attentiveness, I came home from church and freshened up, ready to be swept off my feet again and romanced as we celebrated our year together. Apparently, he missed the memo!

James did not arrive home until 10:00 p.m., tired but happy after going to play tennis with friends from the office. I, meanwhile, had passed from disappointment at his non-arrival to anxiety over his absence. To begin with, he could not understand why I was so mad; we were going to get to spend the whole next day together as we celebrated Independence Day, so what was the big deal? I think I managed to finally get the message across. Certainly, there has never been a repeat incident!

Though I had enjoyed my time with Blue Cross Blue Shield, the work wasn't exactly stretching, and while it was a big office, there did not seem to be a lot of opportunities for advancement. Meanwhile, I had seen how James was finding opportunities through his government-related job, and thought that a similar path may open up some new doors for me.

That is what took me to the downtown Harrisburg office of the Defense Contract Audit Agency, better known as DCAA. There I was greeted by a smiling, round-faced young woman by the name of Nell.

"Oh, you're the new auditor everyone is talking about," she said after I introduced myself. "Come this way."

Nell escorted me back to the branch manager's office, knocked on the door and said with a flourish, "Here's

Juliette." The branch manager stood, shook my hand, and welcomed me to the office. He escorted me to my desk, then took me around the office and introduced me to my new colleagues.

Everyone seemed nice enough, but as I got settled in at my desk, it dawned on me that, other than for Nell at the front desk, I was the only other female in the office of just a dozen or so people—and surrounded by nothing but White Anglo Saxon Protestants. This was very different from my experience at Blue Cross Blue Shield, so I was a little unsure about what to expect, but I didn't want to let my anxiety show.

It wasn't long before my trepidation proved justifiable. Having familiarized myself with the companies we were dealing with, it was determined that I had to make a trip to visit one of my clients. Because I was new to the office and the area, the auditor previously assigned to this client would accompany me on my first visit. Ironically, this first assignment took me back to coal country and reminders of my father's disregard.

Reflecting the ways of the time, it went without saying that the White male colleague with whom I traveled got to select the hotel where we were to stay. He chose a less-than-appealing truck stop because its rates were below the daily per diem we were allotted, allowing him to pocket the difference.

As dinner time approached at the end of our first day in town, I called his room and asked if he was ready to eat: I had to depend on him to drive us to a restaurant because there were no acceptable eating establishments within walking distance of the hotel.

He hesitated for a moment, and then relented. "Okay," he said with a reluctant tone clear in his voice. "Let's go eat."

Things didn't get any more comfortable at the restaurant. During dinner, my co-worker told me that he believed that a woman's place was in the home and not in the workplace. He went on to say that he felt uncomfortable being with me not only because I was a woman, but particularly because I was a Black woman.

I felt so nauseous that I could barely look at my plate. I had thought that I had left that kind of racism behind in the Deep South, but apparently not. Something rose up in me. "I'm sorry you feel that way," I told him as politely but firmly as I could. "But I have been sent here to get a job done, and I am going to stay on it until I have fulfilled my responsibilities." Somehow, I got through the rest of the meal and we drove back to the truck stop in silence.

Only when I was safely in my room, with the door closed behind me, could I finally let my guard down. I collapsed onto the bed in tears.

Regaining my composure, I took a deep breath, then picked up the telephone. I called my colleague's room and told him that henceforth I would ride with him to and from the location of our audit, but that I would no longer accompany him to dinner.

The next morning, we rode to and from the work site in silence. After returning to our hotel, I went to the truck stop convenience store and purchased Vienna sausages, a soft drink and crackers for dinner, eating alone in my room.

Completing our job the following day, we then headed back to Harrisburg. Other than to communicate about our work, we had not spoken since that first evening. He decided to break his silence on the drive home, asking me not to disclose to anyone in the office what had happened during our trip.

I didn't reply, fearful of what he might do if he knew I was planning to report him to our supervisor as soon as I returned to the office. I was acutely aware that any confrontation about that could be dangerous for me—physically, professionally, and even psychologically.

Immediately upon my return to the office, I had a meeting with my supervisor. I was calm and collected but firm. I told him all that had happened, and bluntly requested that I not be assigned another job with that particular co-worker. Given that this was government-related work, I fully expected my request to be treated respectfully and seriously. Therefore, my supervisor's response came as a tremendous shock.

"If I do that, the branch manager might think that there was a problem," he said. His tone and facial expression implied I was complicit in a story that might be much more salacious than the facts I'd presented. I left the office heartbroken, reminded that my race and my gender left me doubly exposed to prejudice.

Some time later I was assigned another out-of-town audit assignment in Wilkes Barre, Pennsylvania; this time with a different White male co-worker. Expecting the worst, I set out with my defenses up, but to my surprise and delight, he was very respectful of me, and we worked well together. He treated me as an equal, and I realized that not all of my colleagues believed that a woman's place was in the home. I decided it was safe to begin to relax a little.

During the audit, my supervisor made an unexpected visit to the site. He arrived late in the day and stayed overnight at the same hotel where my co-worker and I roomed. We all three enjoyed a pleasant dinner together before returning to our rooms. I was encouraged by the idea that perhaps my supervisor was experiencing a change of heart and now saw me as a valuable member of his team—without considering my race or gender.

My thoughts were interrupted by a knock at the door. Peering through the peep hole, I spied my supervisor's face. Surprised by the sudden interruption, I opened the door, and he pushed his way in. A rolling wave of alcohol accompanied him, and immediately I recognized that I was in danger.

Mustering all the strength I could, I pushed him back out over the threshold and slammed the door closed. I double-locked the door, sat down on the floor with my back against it, and caught my breath between my tears.

CHAPTER SIX

THE MORNING AFTER the terrifying encounter with my drunken supervisor, I got dressed, smoothed down my clothes, and took a deep breath. I was going to finish the job come what may. Still shaken, I was relieved when I learned from my co-worker that our supervisor had already departed for the drive back to Harrisburg. I didn't mention what had happened, and we got through the rest of the audit without incident.

Only when I got back to Harrisburg did I let myself feel all that was going on inside. As I told James tearfully what had happened, he was enraged. He had suffered his share of prejudice as a Black man, naturally, but he knew that he didn't face additional vulnerability because of his gender. His anger at the way I had been treated was mixed with a feeling of impotence, too. We both knew that making a formal complaint would be a waste of time. And while I appreciated his desire to go down to the office to have it out with my supervisor man to man, we also knew that wasn't going to be an effective answer.

After mulling it over for a few days, we decided that the best thing to do was to move away. Having done well in his time at the Naval Ships Parts Control Center, James was able to secure a position in Arlington, Virginia, working in Foreign Military Sales, and I managed to arrange a transfer to a DCAA office in the area.

Heading back to where we had come from seemed like a retrograde step, in some ways, taking us nearer to the South we had wanted to leave behind, but we hoped that by moving to a more cosmopolitan area we could avoid some of the horrors we'd experienced in our first post-college stop.

When I arrived at the office on the first day of my new job, I could not believe my eyes. The people working there were young, middle-aged, and older; they were White, Black, Asian, and Indian; they were men and women. All working together. It was a far cry from the all-White-male office I'd left. I immediately relaxed into a workplace comfort I had not previously known. And I was welcomed with open arms as an equal member of the team. I was ready to start a new chapter where I would be judged by my performance rather than incorrect assumptions about my abilities based on race or gender. My sense that I had found a new area of opportunity was confirmed within a month, when I received my first promotion.

It was here too that I also really fell in love with my work. With the largest budget of all the federal agencies, the Department of Defense spent a lot of money, and it was our role in the DCAA to see that it did so as wisely as possible. I considered it a service to both my country and my fellow taxpayers to ensure that government money was being used well; every dollar saved mattered. Over the years, I was able to help save the government many millions of dollars in unnecessary costs, which was very satisfying.

Working as an auditor combined my ability with numbers with my high regard for justice and doing the right thing. Having grown up in an an environment where I had been treated so unfairly, I keenly felt that no one should be taken advantage of. At the same time, I was aware of the responsibility I had to be fair to the contractors, too, as our recommendations regarding their bids determined whether or not they got the work—which in turn impacted their employees, of course.

Reviewing a contractor's proposal was no small task. It could take months, and sometimes involved a team of several of us. We would carefully go through all the company's procedures and policies to ensure the integrity of the costs they were reporting and weed out any "unallowable costs." It was like detective work, painstakingly following all the clues. We wanted to avoid the kind of waste and scandal that would arise from time to time when contractor gouging was revealed in the media, such as the company that charged the Department of Defense $71 for a small pin part for a helicopter that actually cost a mere four cents—a 170,000 percent hike!

Not everyone was deliberately trying to swindle the government, of course. In some cases, it was just that they were careless or simply hadn't followed the rules to the letter. And given the exacting nature of the bidding process, it wasn't hard to make a mistake. That is why we had to go over everything with a fine-toothed comb, asking for clarity or explanations or relevant supporting paperwork whenever we came across an inconsistency or inaccuracy.

Naturally, our presence was not always appreciated. Contractors wanted to be accommodating and helpful, but at the same time they could be a little intimidated by our presence. I ignored any awkwardness and just concentrated on doing my job as well as I could. I was always polite, but clear that I was there to ensure that all government protocols were followed properly.

One time I was leading an audit at a company where I'd had some questions about their paperwork, when there was a knock at the door of the office in which I had been set up for my stay.

I looked up as the owner of the business opened the door and stuck his head in. I smiled and nodded a greeting, and he stepped inside—casually holding a rifle in his hand, as if it were a manila folder.

"Good morning," he said, sitting down across from me and propping the weapon up against the desk. "I just wanted to check that you are getting everything that you need?" He was doing his best to act normal, while sending a sinister silent message.

Though alarm bells may have been going off inside, I was determined not to let him know that. I stared him down. "Yes, thank you," I said. "So far. I'll be sure to let you know if I have any more questions as I go on."

There was a pause as we looked at each other, and then he nodded. "All right, good." He stood up, picked up the rifle, and walked out. I made a note of what had happened, to give to my supervisor when I got back, and went back to work.

• • •

MY CAREER WASN'T the only part of my life in which I determined that the experiences of my childhood would be a springboard to more rather than an anchor forever weighing me down and holding me back. My stepmother's constant criticism, telling me that I would never amount to anything, had fueled my desire to prove her wrong by excelling at work. And when it came to family, I was committed to ensuring that any children we might have would always know they were deeply loved. My stepmother provided the example of exactly what not to do.

Our desire for children wasn't fulfilled easily. Only after several years of trying and some medical intervention did we finally learn I was expecting. We were so excited and so nervous after waiting so long. I remember walking through a busy mall at Christmastime, heavily pregnant, with James holding his arms out in front of me to keep anyone from bumping into me, like a football player running interference.

Much as I wanted to be a mother, my heart had been so full with love for James that I wasn't certain that there would be any space for anyone else. But I realized that fear was horribly unfounded from the first moment I held Ashley in my arms.

From her birth on March 9, 1983, I have endeavored to tell her that I love her every single day. It wasn't just a matter of speaking those words, either— through my actions, I also wanted to show her that our house was one where love prevailed. James and I worked hard to foster a home characterized by love, honesty, and respect. We were guided by the wisdom of Proverbs 22:6, which tells parents, "Train up a child in the way she should go, and when she is old, she will not depart from it."

With that in mind, we applied ourselves to ensuring that Ashley had every opportunity possible to make the most of her God-given talents, which included a love for dance. We nurtured her every day, and constantly reminded her that she was loved. I tried to make sure that I was the mother I had wanted as a child. Ashley reciprocated by never taking us for granted, and by seizing the opportunities we provided and working hard to become a productive citizen, of whom we are very proud.

When she was nine years old, we jointly selected a needy child in Honduras to sponsor through an organization called Children International. While I had known poverty as a child, Ashley had not, and I wanted her to have an impact in lessening the burden on some other young person who was suffering. Throughout her childhood, we kept in touch with this child, and contributed consistently, making a small dent in the world's misfortune.

I was thrilled a few years ago when Ashley came to me and said, "It's time I sponsor my own child." She selected a little boy of her own to support through the same organization. He had the same birthday as her, which created an instant bond. She proudly displays his photograph on her refrigerator door. Every time I see it, I know that I have had a role in creating a better world, and my heart swells with joy in the knowledge that my daughter cares so deeply for others.

We would have loved to have more children, but it just wasn't to be. We even explored adoption for a while, before deciding that was not for us. And while I truly believe that James and I could have loved as many children as God would have given us, my inability to become pregnant and give birth again helped me to realize what an absolute miracle Ashley is.

Every time I look into her eyes I see a bit of myself, but she is also very much her own person. When she was younger, she was an introvert like me, but when she reached her teenage years she burst out of that shell. I don't know whether that is ironic or instructive—when I was fifteen, the actions of my father and stepmother pushed me further back into my shell, whereas at that same age Ashley broke out of hers. I hope that it's a sign that, with loving parenting, each child has the opportunity to become the greatest version of him or herself.

Though I had a strong desire to be the mother for my daughter that I had never had, I knew that wasn't going to be enough on its own. I had some fears that I might inadvertently repeat or mimic some of the horrible behaviors of my father and stepmother, so I applied myself to learning. I read lots of books because I didn't know how to be a good mother from example.

That helped when Ashley began to pull away a little as a teen; though it made me sad, I also recognized that it was an important developmental moment for her, and I needed to give her some space. Understanding what was happening made it easier for me.

Forging her own path has included graduating from Spelman College with a degree in Economics—an aptitude she must have inherited from me—and later earning a Master's in Public Policy from American University. Equally importantly, it has included finding the love of her life, and making James and me grandparents twice over.

When Ashley went off to college, I wrote her a journal full of advice, all the little lessons that I'd accumulated over my lifetime to that point. While she wasn't yet ready to get married at that point, I instructed her that when the time came she should marry a man who loved her more than she loved him.

I didn't mean to imply that she shouldn't love her husband—quite to the contrary, that should be the bedrock of every healthy marriage. But I wanted her to know that she should not accept anything less than complete devotion from a future husband. Years later, she came to me and told me that she was dating a man and that they were getting serious. There was only one unexpected element to this love story—he was White.

I certainly didn't object to Ashley marrying a White man, I had just always envisioned her with someone Black. Having been raised in a segregated environment where people almost exclusively married someone from their own race, it was all I knew.

Any doubts or concerns I may have had about Ashley's choice were completely erased when she told me of Damian, "He treats me better than any man I've ever dated."

I told her, "That's what it's all about. It's more important than any other factor."

Making sure that Ashley had the big wedding day that I did not was a delight, like I was living my own dream at the same time. It made me feel so good to be able to give that to her. And in all the years since, Damian has not disappointed, proving to be a loving and caring husband and father. We couldn't be more pleased for them both. Today Ashley is my best friend; we see each other frequently, and talk on the phone several times a day. I am so grateful for the sweet relationship we enjoy.

I was touched when she came to me after the birth of their first child and asked for an update to the book of advice I had given her when she went off to college. That one was handwritten; this time around I gathered all my thoughts in a specially published one-off book, titled *Mom's Advice for Life*. In it, I passed along all I had learned about personal growth, career advancement, marriage and parenting. I encouraged her to work hard, stand up for herself, and keep focused on what really matters in life—treating others well, being honest, doing your best, and building a loving home and family.

• • •

WHEN JAMES AND I started a new family together, I was also unexpectedly given the opportunity to rebuild some of my old one. One day in 1984, out of the blue, I answered the phone to my sister Emma. She was going to be in the Baltimore area, she told me, and wanted to drop by and visit.

I was stunned. I hadn't heard from any of my older siblings since they had left home some twenty years before, nor been in touch with any of my younger brothers or step-siblings since I had walked away for the last time after graduating. As far as I was aware, we had been lost to each other, like a refugee family separated in a mass exodus. But another story started to emerge, which only deepened my awareness of how much harm Daddy and my stepmother had caused, not just to me but to everyone in the family, in their own way.

During her brief first visit, Emma told me how the rest of the siblings were in contact with each other, mostly in the Detroit area. On one of their get-togethers, our youngest brother Frankie had suggested trying to find me, and Emma had taken up the challenge. So began a series of reunions in which we started to fill in the blanks from all of those missing years, and put together a picture of what had really happened.

While I had not faulted first Emma and then Sarah for leaving home when they could stand it no longer, I had felt a little abandoned by them. What I didn't know was that they had made several attempts to contact me, which had been blocked by Daddy and our stepmother, to invite me to join them in Detroit. For their part, Sarah and Emma felt like I had just forgotten about them.

Nothing could have been farther from the truth. I often wondered where they were and how they were doing. But because I felt such a responsibility to do what I was told by Daddy and my stepmother, even though it was unreasonable, I don't know that I would have had the courage or confidence to have taken my sisters up on their offer, had I learned of it. Nonetheless, hearing that they had attempted to reach out to me was a balm for some of the years of separation; it was good to know that, even though I was unaware of it at the time, there were people who still cared for me. It was also comforting to learn that our family had not been completely scattered; Emma had lived with Barbara at one stage, and Sarah had lived with Emma and her husband for a time.

As we re-established our relationships and learned about each other's lives during all those missing years, it became clear to me that our shared childhood experiences had affected us all, though in different ways. I learned about bouts of depression and tough times they had endured. There were more than a few tears as we talked through all that had happened.

One time when we were all together at Frankie's home in the early years of our reconnection, Frankie brought Daddy over to visit. If I'd hoped for some sort of reconciliation, I was disappointed. He stayed for only an hour or so and it was like the clock had been turned back decades; he was quiet and detached. He neither asked about our lives, nor volunteered anything about his own. When the conversation drifted to the hard times when we were younger, he just said that we all needed to forgive and forget. No suggestion that he needed to ask for forgiveness, no hint of remorse or admission of wrongdoing was forthcoming.

Over the years since we siblings reunited, some relationships have been repaired more than others. After a period in which we were in contact, I am no longer connected to my older half-sister, Barbara. I am sad about that, because she is one of the links I share to Momma, but I remain grateful to her for providing a safe space for Emma and when she fled the home. Without Barbara's help, the family may have been further splintered.

Emma now lives in Rome, Georgia, where her caring and nurturing nature remains unchanged. In addition to a career in nursing, she has been active in her church and in the local community. Perhaps because of what she experienced growing up, she has had a particular concern for families, serving on several committees involved in court issues related to children's welfare.

Sarah suffered at home for her spirited personality, but found comfort in her faith as a Jehovah's Witness on moving away. Though we were quite different in our demeanor, since reconnecting we have found how similar we are in many other ways—so much so that James has joked we are twins separated by two years.

Both being left-handers is part of the bond, but it goes much further. On my first visit to her home in Mount Pleasant, Michigan, I was astonished to find Sarah had the same wall frieze as we did. I learned, too, that we shared an appreciation for duck memorabilia, and were each the financial scorekeepers in our home.

Sadly, I didn't get to reconnect with John. I never saw my younger brother from the day he left home with Sarah. He was raised by relatives in the Detroit area and joined the military, serving in Vietnam. Returning to the United States, he turned to drugs to deal with his experiences while at war, and was later diagnosed as paranoid schizophrenic. He spent most of the rest of his life in and out of veteran hospitals and private homes until his death on September 24, 2017, having only intermittent contact with Emma and Sarah, who checked up on him as best they could. Attending the memorial service for him, I did not feel any deep grief, sadly, because I had never really known him; more, I mourned the fact we had been strangers.

Physically, Frankie reminds me of my father, which is somewhat disconcerting, as is his memory of Daddy as being a great man. But, then, I realize that he had something of a different upbringing. There may not have been much affection, but there was certainly more freedom for him, as a boy, than I had enjoyed. And I am forever thankful to Frankie for being the catalyst in bringing the family back together in some measure.

We will never be like television's the Cleavers or the Huxtables, but we have found our way back to each other in varying degrees, for which I am so grateful. I was concerned that the career and financial success James and I have enjoyed might be a source of tension, but that has never been the case. We'll all meet up at least once a year for some time together, when there will be lots of hanging out in the kitchen as we prepare food, catching up. We just don't talk about the past much; some things are best left unsaid.

CHAPTER SEVEN

I DON'T KNOW that I will ever be able to say that I am grateful for my difficult childhood experiences, but I can look back on them now with a level of appreciation for the way they became a catalyst in my life. Much of what I have enjoyed in my career and my personal life came as a result of determining that Daddy and my stepmother would not have the last word.

Her repeated shaming and declaring that I would never amount to anything lit a fire that burned under me throughout my working life. I was determined to prove her—and anyone else who might agree—wrong. I may not be more capable than everyone else, but I could work longer and harder. Countless hours doing chores around the house had conditioned me to long days without a break.

I was well aware that, as a Black woman, any advances I achieved would only be on merit. That is why, when during my time with Blue Cross Blue Shield, I was able to shrug it off when a male colleague griped one time that I had taken the promotion that was his. I knew that it had gone to me because of my better performance, and I didn't let his negativity get to me.

That was the attitude that saw me through a steady rise in rank and responsibility during my twenty-five-year government career. It took me from the DCAA to the Department of the Navy, where I helped run the data processing group from offices in the historic Washington Navy Yard. From there, I moved on to the Department of Defense Comptroller's Office at the Pentagon, and finally the Environmental Protection Agency (EPA), from which I retired in 2003.

It was there, in my most senior role as the first Black woman to be appointed Director of Finance, overseeing a multi-billion-dollar budget, that I learned my subordinates had a secret nickname for me: Tiger Lady. I wasn't offended by it, rather I took it as a quiet compliment—recognition that I was there to get the job done.

If ever I felt I had finally proved my stepmother wrong, it may have been when I was selected to join the Federal Government Senior Executive Service, the highest level attainable for civilian employees, chosen for their leadership abilities. Our task was to serve as a bridge between political appointees heading different federal agencies and their branch personnel. As a result, I found myself in many high-level meetings, dealing with senior officials and colossal budgets.

One achievement of which I was particularly proud was in my final position, at the EPA, when we earned a "green" rating from the White House for passing audits with flying colors in two consecutive years, and beating a deadline for completing a major report by a full twelve months. It was a proud moment for our team.

Maintaining that sort of standard required a high level of commitment, naturally. I would often put in ten-hour days—head down, with no time for small talk or idling of any kind—and then bring work home to do later in the evening. Naturally, this meant teamwork on the home front was essential.

James was a tremendous support and encouragement in all of this, even as he dealt with career demands of his own. When we moved to Virginia, he began traveling internationally with his work. Switching from government employment to a contractor, he later became frustrated by some of the processes he had to deal with and felt that he could do more on his own.

I knew he was capable, but it was still something of a step of faith to leave the security of a steady paycheck and start his own business. In the early stages there were better years and not so good ones, and the pressures increased when James also went back to school to get his MBA. But over time his professionalism, personality, persuasiveness, and persistence began to pay off in ways that we could never have imagined.

By the time James retired and sold his company, it had grown from a one-man operation started in our attic to an international operation with some thirty-five-hundred employees in twenty-plus states and a dozen countries. I'm so proud of all he has achieved, while remaining the same kind and unassuming person he has always been.

Somehow we managed to make both demanding careers work. Ensuring that Ashley grew up in a home where she knew she was loved was a high priority for both of us, so we juggled things to be certain one of us was always there for her.

With his office being closer to home, James was able to adjust his schedule to take Ashley to preschool and later grade school, while I made the commute into Washington, DC. Afternoons he might collect her and take her back with him to his office, where she would do homework, and I would have time with them when I got back before putting her to bed and then picking up on my work again. We just did whatever it took.

We also learned to blend our strengths and personalities. Neither of us had seen a healthy marriage modeled in our home—James because of bereavement, I because of abuse. I don't know what drew Daddy and my stepmother to one another. Maybe it was more a match of convenience than anything else; Momma's death had left him as a single father to six children, and she had three sons of her own, with no man for support. Certainly, I never remember ever seeing any tenderness between the two of them; the only intimate interaction between them was crude, when Daddy would grab his crotch and gesture to my stepmother, making it clear that he expected to have sex later that day. I would cringe every time I saw him do that.

We may not have had good examples to copy, but James and I loved each other and were determined we would make our relationship work. So we grew up together, learning and working things out.

One thing I appreciated about James was his commitment to being a good father, having grown up without one of his own and knowing how that absence affects you. And of course I wanted my daughter to know the love and protection of a father that I'd missed. So I loved the little ways James would express that, like walking on the outside when we were in the street, between us and the traffic, like a gentleman of old. Over time, his kindness and warmth of character helped to erase the hurt caused by my father's coldness.

Financial security was important to us from the beginning. When we met, neither of us owned much more than the clothes on our backs and the few things we had brought with us to Alabama State. We had nothing to fall back on and no one to turn to to bail us out if things went wrong, so we were conservative when it came to spending.

Whenever we were faced with a significant financial decision, I'd bring my accounting strengths to the table and ask about the "cost-benefit analysis," so much so that it became something of a catchphrase for us. I believe that doing all we could to minimize financial stress helped the rest of our relationship bloom. And talking openly about money encouraged communication in other areas, too.

By the time we came to buy our first home in Virginia, between us we were well able to afford the modest mortgage payments, but it was still a scary decision to commit to that level of a loan.

• • •

AMONG THE MEMORABILIA from my government career is a framed copy of the stars and stripes that was flown over the Pentagon in my honor when I retired on November 22, 2003. The recognition was special, as were the many different medals, plaques, and other honors I received, including a letter of commendation from President George W. Bush.

The truth is, however, that to some degree I now consider that my priorities were rather mixed up. I am glad for what I was able to achieve in my work, but I now know that is not where I have found my true peace and value. The financial security we have known has been a blessing, but it is relationships that have proved to be the most meaningful thing in life.

I have been fortunate to travel and enjoy some of the good things in life, but all that doesn't matter nearly as much as your family and your friends. Friends help to clarify life, soothe your fears, and encourage you when you are down. They'll stand by your side when life throws you challenges, visit you when you are sick, and celebrate your achievements with you. And when your time is over on this earth, true friends will remember you and lighten the spirit with memories of joyous times spent together.

If I have a regret, it is that I did not recognize this earlier. As it was, my naturally introverted personality and my focus on succeeding at work meant that I did not invest as much in other relationships as I now see I perhaps should have done. So I cherish even more those I have developed.

The friendship with Vivian that was born the day we met in the entrance to Abercrombie Hall has lasted even until now, forty-plus years later. No matter how much our lives have changed since that first day, I know that I have her support and she will always have mine. We see each other at least once or twice a year and she looks the same as she did on that first meeting. Time has been very kind to her, and I consider her a true friend.

Then there is Lula. She and I met after James and I moved to the Washington, DC, area and began looking for a church home. We settled at Alfred Street Baptist Church in Alexandria, Virginia, an historic Black congregation dating back to 1803 that was started by slaves from George Washington's plantation, and which had a reputation for being spiritually vibrant and socially active. Among its many ministries are a homeless shelter and low-income housing. We soon met people with whom we made friends, and I established a deep connection with one in particular.

Lula was a gentle soul, with a heart for children that made her perfectly suited for her job as a school librarian. She had a daughter the same age as Ashley, and because our girls were involved in lots of church-related activities, I saw her often. Our friendship has grown over the course of nearly forty years, and even though our girls are long grown and out of college and have drifted apart, the bond that Lula and I share is as strong as ever.

We get together for lunch at least once a month, when we openly laugh, cry, complain about and celebrate the various things going on in our lives. After Vivian, she became the second person who I would consider a true and lifelong friend.

Through my connections at church, I've developed several other very strong and committed relationships. We share some of the same values and have similar interests in politics, community affairs, and cultural activities. The depth of those friendships varies in intensity, but even in regard to those whose houses I've never visited to share a meal, I know that I can count on them for good discussions about family and other things that interest us.

Though they have both since passed away, Gladys and Millie also taught me much about friendship. They "adopted" first James and then me too with no motivation other than having big hearts. Being considerably older than we were, it wasn't as though we shared similar interests or life challenges, they simply saw that we were alone and welcomed us into their circle. They would invite us over for meals, or invite themselves over if they were going to be in our area! When they discovered we did not have enough spare chairs to seat everyone, they brought us some which we have continued to use to this day. Each time we bring them out for guests, I am reminded of the example of our surrogate mothers.

Before they died, Gladys and Millie were among just a handful of special guests invited when James and I celebrated our twenty-fifth wedding anniversary by renewing our vows at Alfred Street Baptist Church. We made sure our two "moms" rode in a limo of their own this time. Meanwhile, I got to wear a real wedding dress, and James presented me with a new ring. It's much more visually impressive than the one he gave me in 1976, but that first one remains priceless to me.

As I grew older, I began to recognize that I had fewer close friends than many other women, and that I had filled the empty spot in my heart where friends may have been with a relentless drive for professional achievement. I wish I could say that, after this revelation, I developed lots of new friendships, but I didn't.

Sometimes I wish I could be more outgoing, like James, but I remain an introvert and I know that's unlikely to change at this point. I recognize that when people get to know me they realize I am friendly and loving, but I still fear that my shyness sometimes comes off as being unfriendly. Nevertheless, I am working on it. It is never too late to discover new friends and nurture those relationships.

While I may not have many close friendships, I've realized that the best ones develop when you are open to the possibilities. I have learned that some friends come into your life for a reason and others come about rather unexpectedly. They may live in your neighborhood, attend your church, or have been in your life undiscovered for years. Even your relatives can become your friends, bound together in relationships far thicker than blood.

I've learned that friends are a valuable part of life, whether you have two close friends or two hundred, and it's important to appreciate what they bring into your life and give the same in return.

•••

THROUGHOUT THE MANY years I strove to outperform my peers at all costs, I was unable to recognize that I was allowing my past to affect me in such an unhealthy way. There was some jealousy on the part of some of my peers as I collected various commendations, but at the time, I considered that their problem, not mine.

I was not aware that my childhood experiences had not only spurred me to do well, but that I had let them make me become driven; I was an overachiever. The constant negativity from Daddy and my stepmother had left me feeling that there must be something wrong with me, that I was deficient somehow, and that I needed to make up for that in some way to be acceptable and accepted. As a result, I'd embraced a flawed pecking order of priorities that started with my career, then moved to my family, while somewhere far below sat my friends.

Looking back, I can now see I wasted too much time suffering from and being affected by the early losses in my life, I unwittingly allowed them to snowball into even more losses, like my diminished capacity for friendships. Fortunately, it's never too late to fix a situation like that, and as a grown woman I finally realized that I needed to let go of the things that I could not change or control—and leave the past in the past. This was a major, life-changing breakthrough.

Unlikely as it sounds, it came during a professional development seminar. Though I consistently excelled at work, it was not a happy sort of success; I always felt the need to prove myself in a professional environment, to show that I wasn't the young girl who'd been told she'd amount to nothing. That tended to alienate many people. Even in my forties, without being aware of it, I still maintained the adversarial relationship that I'd had with my stepmother. Long after I thought she was out of my life, she continued to live in my mind and affect my actions.

Then I attended a seminar on stress management and effective ways to accept change. The presenter stated that if something changed and you could not control it, you should let it go. It was such a simple statement, but it was like a light-bulb went on in my head, a true epiphany. I saw immediately how I could apply this concept to my personal life, and I vowed to myself that I would do so.

I wanted to let go of the pain and insecurity that had subtly defined my life up until that point, but it wasn't easy because there were many layers of hurt to peel back. The loss of my mother, my father's distance, and my stepmother's cruelty were all hugely significant factors in my unhappiness, but they weren't the only ones. As a Black woman, I was also aware that some of my doubts were the legacy of being raised in the African American culture and judged by Whites pursuant to a set of ethnocentric and semi-arbitrary standards. Meanwhile, African American women had an additional cross to bear, being both judged and demeaned by many men.

As if all this were not enough, there was yet an additional wrinkle. I needed to acknowledge a further uncomfortable but unavoidable reality: to be a Black woman in America means that you are often judged by women as well, and the most demanding judges many times are other Black women. It's an unfortunate truth, but it's a fact of life that we live with every day. What should be the greatest source of our solidarity is often where we are most exposed and left alone. No matter how much we'd like to think that we'd empathize with those who share our experiences, in many instances we are judged most harshly by those who are most like us.

After listening to and truly digesting that seminar speaker's simple truths, I began to work diligently to let my insecurities go. While I suffered through many indignities and losses during my childhood, the greatest challenge occurred when Momma died. Her death was outside of my control, but it ate at me. When my father subsequently remarried, and my siblings left home, I likewise had no control over the situation.

Only many decades later did I realize that I'd spent my life allowing others to control me. It's never too late to reclaim the power within you—a power that I didn't know I had—and that simple decision changed everything for me. It hasn't been easy, but I'm proud to say that as a Black woman now in my sixties I have achieved some level of peace with myself. I am older and wiser, and being judged by men or women of whatever color is no longer important to me. Their acceptance no longer defines me. What matters more to me now is how God sees and judges me.

No longer do I allow my past experiences to define me, limit me, or control me. It was a personal choice that I needed to make, and it has been liberating. I feel lighter and happier than I could have ever imagined. Instead of looking back regretting all the time I lost, I now look ahead to new possibilities.

Part of the process has involved letting go of things that I can't change in others or about others. Some relationships can't be fixed no matter how much I would like it to be otherwise; there comes a time when you just have to move on, even when it involves family.

I thought I had left Daddy and my stepmother behind once and for all when I returned to Montgomery, after my brief return home on graduation, but James encouraged me to make one more effort at some sort of reconnection not long after we were married. He believed family was important and wondered whether my experiences could truly have been as bad as they sounded.

We visited Brighton on two occasions, neither time being received warmly nor having any interest expressed in how we were doing as we tried to make our way in the world. When we subsequently sent some money to help them through a financial hard time without hearing anything, James acknowledged that, yes, it was time to let go.

"You know, Juliette," he told me, "I could tell that your experiences with your stepmother had been hard on you, but I wasn't sure she had been as bad as you said. Turns out you were right. Having gotten to meet her and observe her, I realize that she wasn't as bad as you said—she was worse!"

In the years that followed our sibling reunion, I would occasionally hear a little about Daddy and our stepmother, but I never inquired. I knew that as Daddy aged, he suffered from ill health as a result of his hard job and hard drinking. His physical problems included diabetes that ultimately required the amputation of both his legs, leaving him bedridden. I wish I could say that it saddened me to hear that, but it truly didn't; it was simply something that happened to a stranger, as far as I was concerned.

I was shocked, however, to learn of his death on February 15, 2003—though mostly because of the manner in which the news came to me. I took a phone call from Emma, telling me that our stepmother had been in touch asking for money to help pay for Daddy's funeral. This was why our stepmother was making contact—because of finances, not family connection.

But when Frankie called the funeral home to inquire about the costs, the man there told him that Daddy's burial had been paid for by a policy our father had taken out years before. Not only that, but our stepmother knew about it because she had taken the policy paperwork to the funeral home, the man said. Even in death, it seemed, we were being manipulated.

Nonetheless, I felt it was only proper to attend the funeral, to show a token of respect: Sometimes it is important just to do the right thing. Daddy had given me life, even if he had not then attempted to give me much of one. My stepmother did not greet or acknowledge us, nor were we invited to join her and the others at the graveside. When I learned a couple of years later that she had died, I did not go back for her funeral.

CHAPTER EIGHT

NEGATIVE EXPERIENCES CAN become a catalyst for positive change, if we will let them. That was true for me not only in regards to allowing the rejection and belittling I endured as a child to become fuel to drive me to succeed, but also in the area of generosity. Together, the personal experience of what it is like to struggle financially, the gracious way Ernestine responded when I was caught stealing from her made me a giver for the rest of my life.

Though we had always given to our church as part of our commitment to tithing, James and I reached a place where we felt we were in a position to increase our financial generosity and became aware of opportunities to make an impact in the broader community. Interestingly, our first such move actually came through church. I was serving as a trustee at Alfred Street Baptist Church when we began to explore the idea of extending our community service by starting a preschool program. Before doing so, however, we agreed to see what similar services might already exist that we could come alongside, rather than needlessly reinventing the wheel. That brought us to Hopkins House.

Founded in 1939, the nonprofit organization had a long and distinguished history in providing education programs for mostly low-income, working families in the Alexandria area. Through the years its child development and family learning work had attracted a string of notable visitors, including then-Illinois Senator Barack Obama, renowned pediatric surgeon Ben Carson, and then-Virginia Governor Tim Kaine.

We visited the center, and I was immediately moved by the mothers I met there. In their struggle, I could see my own experience, as well as that of many of the people with whom I was raised. Most of the women there were hard workers, trying as best they could to make a better life for themselves and their children. They didn't want a handout, but rather a helping hand to raise them up to a better life.

Impressed by what we saw, and passionate about the difference a good education can make, James and I signed up as volunteers, getting to visit classes and work with the students. In time, we also began to help raise money for this valuable community service.

When Hopkins House later built a new center in a community where we had lived many years earlier, we knew we wanted to help.

In this new facility, the children are in small classes where they are exposed to things that they wouldn't otherwise learn about. It ensures that they get off to a good start in life—the type I did not have. While it didn't handicap me in the long run, for many other similarly situated young people, a rough start can be difficult if not impossible to overcome. I had also suffered my greatest youthful embarrassments in a schoolhouse setting, so it seemed poetic to me that the place where I could give back the most would be a school.

Attending the first graduation of the new James L. and Juliette McNeil Preschool, as I watched nineteen of the most precious, adorable children walk down the aisle in caps and gowns, I could see immense potential in every one of them. Each of them might be a future doctor, lawyer, executive, scientist, teacher, politician, and, of course, parent. Their opportunities were limitless.

As I watched the graduates' little hands reach for their diplomas and turn proudly to their parents with big smiles on their faces, I realized how far I had traveled from Country Club Drive. Rather than dwell on the fact that I'd never had a loving mother to look up to during happy times—in fact there had been few happy times at all—I was caught up in the joy I got to share in.

Making a difference in the lives of these children from low-income families and all those that have followed them has been one of the most rewarding experiences of my life. Some people would say that I've given them a tremendous gift, but I've been so blessed in life that the opportunity to help others is not only my calling, it is also truly a gift to my heart.

Helping young children establish good learning habits has been gratifying, but we have also invested in older students. Even with a solid educational foundation, some young adults are not going to be able to achieve their full potential without additional financial help.

One way we have helped here is by establishing a scholarship foundation at Alabama State that assists qualifying students with their school fees. In addition, we also support Alfred Street Baptist Church's scholarship program, which is open to applications from anyone in the community, not just church members.

Typically, we don't hear from recipients and that is fine. We are not looking for a thank-you; knowing we have been able to help others who are in similar situations to those we came through is reward enough in itself. But on one occasion, I got to see firsthand the impact we have been able to help make.

The doorbell rang one morning, and I opened the door to a young woman standing there holding a bouquet of flowers. She handed them to me and explained that our financial support had made it possible for her to leave home and attend college. Not only had this opened up new doors of opportunity for her, it had also been a rescue, in some ways; she had been sexually abused by her stepfather, she said, and had not known how to get away from her tormentor. Though that had not been my direct experience, I could readily identify with how she felt trapped in mistreatment, so to see her free and looking forward to a bright future moved me to tears.

Because of our backgrounds in business and accounting, James and I believe in investing our philanthropic money wisely, so we usually give to well-established programs. However, on one occasion I was spurred to react rather more emotionally.

I was leafing through a copy of *U.S. News & World Report* magazine's annual college rankings report when I was astonished to see that Alabama State's graduation rate was only twenty-four percent, much lower than all the other similar schools. I could not believe what I was reading; how could only one in four students be successfully completing their schooling? Something must be seriously wrong. I had to get to the bottom of it.

Picking up the phone, I called the school and got passed along to someone who could help me. The explanation both reassured and enraged me. The low graduation rate was not a reflection of academic achievements, I was told, but economic failures—if a student had an outstanding balance, no matter how small, and no matter how successful they might have been in their studies, they could not obtain their diploma.

I was furious. College had saved my life; it had been my way out. Here were young people being held back simply because of what could be a small debt. It just seemed so wrong. I asked how many students were not graduating that year because they had some unmet school bill and was told there were 105 of them. Then I asked how much money was owed in total, and quickly wrote out a check for the full amount, insisting that the outstanding student debts be paid off anonymously.

•••

NEITHER JAMES NOR I have a need for the spotlight. The satisfaction we get is truly in knowing that we have been able to help people in similar situations to those we once faced, and we are not looking for public acknowledgment. So it took some persuading for us to allow our names to be attached to some of the donations we have made, like Hopkins House.

But then I heard Beverly Tatum, then-President of Spelman College, the oldest historically Black college for women in the country, talk about how it was important to leave some sort of a public legacy, because doing so could inspire or encourage others to follow your example.

We could see some wisdom in that, so we agreed to accept a higher profile in some of our giving. Indeed, in due course our McNeil Family Foundation would be included in the list of "Top 20 Philanthropists of Color" in *Inside Philanthropy* magazine, alongside the likes of Oprah Winfrey, Tyler Perry, Beyoncé, LeBron James, and Will and Jada Pinkett Smith. We still don't feel comfortable with the attention, but we accept it as a way of helping multiply our efforts.

Among the things that now bear our name is a waiting room at INOVA Fairfax Hospital in Fairfax, Virginia, and two nurse stations located in the new tower at INOVA Mount Vernon Hospital in Alexandria, Virginia, not far from where we live. This is a rare departure from our usual emphasis on giving to educational projects and programs because we know how important schooling is.

James first became aware of the hospital need from his work on a couple of its committees. While most people think of hospitals as well-funded institutions that make a lot of money, we discovered that INOVA was a not-for-profit organization that also provided millions and millions of dollars in free indigent services each year. As a result, its development opportunities were limited. With our assistance, the hospital was able to upgrade its inadequate waiting room facilities in the heart center, providing a more comfortable space for relatives to wait and consult with doctors as their loved ones went through surgery. We were pleased to be able to help provide a better environment for people dealing with such stressful situations.

Giving money that has made a difference in other people's lives has been rewarding, but we have also sought to give of our time and talents, not just what we earned for them. I particularly felt an urgency about helping young people make wise decisions about their education, knowing how critical that was in their being able to make a meaningful life for themselves.

It dismayed me to see how many Black students just seemed to drift into college without a real plan for what they wanted to do and what they needed to focus on to achieve it. I remembered how critical the advice I had received about changing my major had been, putting me on the right track. Yet, through my involvement with the church scholarship program, I came across many students who had no real idea about what they should be majoring in. This wasn't altogether surprising, given that many were the first in their families to consider going on to further their education, so no one had any experience in dealing with what could be a bewildering application process. I remembered my own naivete in applying to just one school, though mercifully things had worked out well for me.

I got involved in speaking to high school students and their parents, helping prepare them for a successful college experience. I would suggest they take a simple personality test of one kind or another to help them determine what kind of career might suit them best. I would talk about how they needed to be looking ahead to see where the job markets were trending and what the growing fields would be as they were graduating in a few years' time. I warned them that they needed to press their high school counselors to be sure they were offering good advice. I would tell them about the young woman James and I met one time when she was waiting on our table at a restaurant.

As we got talking, she told us that she had majored in psychology but was frustrated that she had been unable to find a job. She didn't know that an advanced degree was a must in that field—a simple piece of information someone should have given her before she invested so much time and money in her studies. I was disappointed for her but also irritated to think that she had been so badly let down by the system that had not adequately prepared her.

Times have changed a bit since I graduated. These days, in the broader culture, a degree is not as much of a requirement in some fields as it used to be. But that's not true when it comes to African Americans, sadly; ongoing inequality means that a young Black person probably still needs a degree for a door to possibly open, whereas a White student could be considered without one.

• • •

THE ENDEAVOR TO which we have given our most public support is another that is not directly related to academic schooling, though it is certainly highly educational in its own way.

James and I did not really know what to expect when we were invited to the home of very dear friends who shared our interest in giving back to the community. Living in the Washington, DC metropolitan area and being of means, we not infrequently found ourselves being approached on behalf of some of the movers, shakers, and wannabes drawn to the city. All we were told was that our friends wanted us to meet someone special.

He was Lonnie Bunch III. The name did not ring any bells—he was neither a politician or an actor, nor the CEO of a major corporation—but once he started speaking, he captured our attention. For the next ninety minutes we were captivated by the story he told of a place needed to present what he called "A People's Journey, A Nation's Story."

Mr. Bunch was the Director of the Smithsonian National Museum of African American History and Culture, an organization that existed primarily on paper and in the hearts and minds of a few people in the Washington, DC, area and around the country. Established by an Act of Congress, the museum was envisioned as the only one of its kind devoted exclusively to documenting African American life, history, and culture. Mr. Bunch said that it would take hundreds of millions of dollars to make this dream a reality, but he did not ask for contributions that night, he just sowed the seeds. James and I left thrilled by the vision of a place that might capture some of the unique, rich history of Black America. Shortly afterward, we met a woman by the name of Margaret Turner who worked in the Smithsonian's Development Office. Over the course of several weeks of working with her, we decided that we wanted to become Founding Donors of the museum. We had no clue what that meant, but with her sweet-sounding southern drawl Margaret educated us on what was required to build such a monument to the struggles and legacy of a people so often forgotten and ignored. As she laid out the framework of the establishment of the museum and explained the impact that it would have on the nation, and even the world, there was no way that we could not be a part of this momentous endeavor.

Not only did we become Founding Donors, making a one-million-dollar donation to the cause, we also worked to help Margaret cultivate additional donors. The first recruits we turned to were Ashley and Damian, who both were very enthusiastic to become part of the project; a plaque hangs in the museum acknowledging their donation. Following in our footsteps, Ashley also has committed to giving her alma mater, Spelman College, one million dollars over a ten-year period. So far, as of this writing, she has given $400,000 of her pledge. After considerable consultation with the leadership of our congregation, Alfred Street Baptist Church followed our support for the National Museum of African American History and Culture, becoming the first church ever in the long history of the Smithsonian to donate a million dollars.

Being at the museum on September 24, 2016 for its official opening was a moving experience. We joined Presidents Obama and George W. Bush and many of those who like us had given to the project. Despite my reticence about publicity, I was proud to see our name on display as two of the benefactors who had helped bring the museum to life.

We have returned more than a dozen times since then to tour the different exhibitions across five floors. Each time I discover something new about the past to both grieve and be thankful for, from the terrible injustices visited upon African Americans like the 1955 murder of fourteen-year-old Emmett Till in Glendora, Mississippi, to the example and contribution of campaigners and reformers like Dr. Martin Luther King Jr. I always leave both sobered and inspired, aware of how easily prejudice can manifest but also awed by the ways in which it has been overcome. On a personal note, it is a joy to get to see a video about how Alfred Street Baptist Church has contributed to the Washington, DC community over the years, including footage of our choir's joyful singing.

I wish that every American, whatever their color, could experience the National Museum of African American History and Culture, because this chapter of our past is for the most part untaught in our public schools. I believe that educating all of us more about the Black experience would go a long way toward ensuring a more just and accepting society. To that end, I am so glad that James and I have been able to be part of providing a place that takes an unflinching look back but also points the way forward.

While we have been fortunate to be able to make sizable contributions to some endeavors, most of our giving has been on a much smaller scale. It is no less fulfilling, though, recognizing that lesser sums going to small community-based organizations can make a big difference.

Just as most of our charitable contributions have been to educational endeavors, so most of our giving has been to domestic concerns. Other than for projects and programs at our alma mater, or in the communities where we grew up, it has largely been focused on the area where we live. We believe in some way that, as a result, we are seeking to be good neighbors.

We do recognize that we are also part of a global community, though. Through our church's support of the Lott Carey Foundation, we got to visit Liberia, which the former slave-turned-missionary—in whose name the charity was founded—helped establish as an independent nation. With our previous experience in supporting educational projects, we wanted to see how we might help with the school that the foundation helps support.

James offered some suggestions for how the school might become more self-supporting, including the idea of using some of its land to generate income from a rubber tree plantation. Meanwhile I was able to offer my accounting and organizational experience to help smooth school operations. We also provided some computers and a generator—basic equipment that was in seriously short supply.

Liberia's lush, green landscape reminded us of southern Georgia's flatlands and savannas. It was gratifying to be able to help, but also overwhelming in some ways. I knew about hardship in America, certainly, but this was of a different level. To see people struggling without the most basic of resources was heartbreaking. We have not managed to return to Liberia yet, but we continue to support some overseas projects.

CHAPTER NINE

BECAUSE OF BOTH my shuttered upbringing and my retiring nature, I was something of a late bloomer in most areas of my life, including education and romance. But nowhere has that been more true than when it comes to politics. If arriving at Alabama State opened up new horizons in my personal life, they did not really expand in regards to the world at large and issues like race and economics until many years later.

It is not that I was completely unaware politically. The campus protests that had rocked many American universities in the early seventies were a thing of the past by the time I arrived in Montgomery, but change was still in the air. However, as a relatively secluded and small Black campus—with just a handful of White students, who were accepted more as a novelty than a meaningful presence—ours was not a particularly activist school. In fact, I felt safer and more secure there than I ever had back home.

For me, it was more that politics seemed to be an alien world, one dominated by men in general and White men in particular, and therefore not welcoming for women in general and Black women in particular. This view of politics as something involving other people who moved in circles beyond mine had been reinforced by the lack of engagement I saw in my home as I grew up.

Daddy neither commented on what was happening in the wider world, nor tried to help us make sense of what we saw in the news. His silence was a sort of surrender, giving the impression that it was all beyond his—and, by default, our—ability to influence in any way. As far as I am aware, he never voted. Things just were the way they were, and that was that.

On top of all that, as a child I was also consumed with much more parochial concerns—how to navigate my way each day through the uncertain world of Daddy and my stepmother, striving to avoid doing anything that might set them off and make already bad things even worse.

In the years that followed, there were some moments in which the example of Black women gaining some entry into the halls of power made an impact. I remember New York's Shirley Chisholm becoming, in 1968, the first Black woman elected to the United States Congress. I can still hear in my mind some of the incredible speeches given by Barbara Jordan, the first African American woman elected to the Texas Senate after Reconstruction, and the first Southern African American woman elected to the United States House of Representatives.

Later, I recall the sense of connection I felt when Condoleezza Rice was appointed as the first African American woman Secretary of State. Like me, she was from the Birmingham area and had grown up in the segregated South, though there the similarities ended. Her privileged upbringing including piano lessons and private schools was a far cry from my experience, but our shared roots made me proud to claim the association with her. Birmingham had long been a symbol of some of the South's worst legacies of racism, but now its sons and daughters could be proud because the city was being portrayed in a positive light.

As the decades progressed it was clear that there was a slow but steady change in our representation; more Blacks were getting a seat at the table. Yet despite that awareness, I just wasn't motivated or inspired to become more directly involved in politics.

To be honest, due to my uninformed upbringing I was still mostly unaware of how the system worked. Like most Black people, I generally supported the Democratic ticket, primarily because its platform seemed fairer to me and more likely to help the downtrodden and underrepresented. The Republicans, it seemed to me, had become the party of old White men.

The catalyst for my late-in-life political involvement came as George W. Bush neared the end of his presidency. One of those seeking the nomination for the Democratic ticket came to speak at a fundraiser for the Alexandria-area preschool James and I were involved in supporting through our church. Like others, this Senator was accepting any opportunity he could to raise his profile among those in the Washington, DC area who might be of influence and help.

I was impressed by what I saw in and heard from the striking young Black senator from Illinois, who James and I got to meet and speak with during his time at the Hopkins House event. Barack Obama struck me as not only exceptionally eloquent and educated, but also genuine—warm, kind, and truly empathetic to the plights of all Americans.

Nevertheless, the idea that there might actually be a Black president during my lifetime still seemed far-fetched. I know that my parents wouldn't have believed it even if they saw it with their own eyes, given all of the institutional racism that they had experienced in the Deep South.

Impressive as he was, Barack Obama wasn't the only one who inspired me. Truth be told, the real impetus for my entry into the high-charged and fast-paced world of politics was his wife, Michelle. While I can't put my finger on exactly what it was about her that lured me in, I am confident that a huge part of it was that I could see a version of myself in her eyes. She was a wife, a mother, and a career woman, and she was exceptional and exquisite in each of those roles.

When Barack Obama secured the Democratic nomination, while there's no doubt that I was excited by the prospect of having a Black man as President of the United States, somehow I was even more galvanized at the thought of seeing a Black woman as the First Lady of the United States.

While I may have been a late arrival to the political scene, once there I threw myself into it. Never having previously paid much attention to political television coverage before, I quickly became an MSNBC junkie, somewhat to James's surprise. He would wake at 3:00 a.m. to find me watching the latest reports and listening to the political pundits pontificating about this or that as it related to the race for the White House.

Now that I was politically awakened, I became distinctly aware that we were at a pivotal time in the history of our country. I worked diligently to help get Barack Obama elected President, donating to his election campaign, attending fundraisers, and enlisting others to support his candidacy. James and I hosted a number of events in our home and did what we could to encourage our friends and peers to also throw their weight behind the campaign.

On election night, I cried tears of joy as I danced around the house in pure delight after it was announced that Barack Obama was the new President-elect of the United States of America. Despite my devout attention to every aspect of the political process in the months leading up to election day, I hadn't truly believed that it would happen until the final results were presented. As we celebrated, I was filled with a renewed sense of hope not just for the people of the United States, but for people all around the world.

• • •

BARACK OBAMA'S ELECTION victory was not the end of my political involvement. Because of our behind-the-scenes efforts during the campaign, James and I were invited to become members of the Presidential Inaugural Finance Committee, an appointment that combined my new political awareness with my long-time abilities in financial management. It was an honor and a privilege to have the opportunity to contribute, and I took it as a serious responsibility to be part of overseeing the forthcoming celebrations for such an historic time.

During weekly phone calls to the committee for updates on our work, the President-elect would humbly and sincerely thank us for our efforts, and even though we were on a conference call with many people on the line I always felt that he was speaking directly to me. No doubt everyone else felt the same way; that was part of his incredible magnetism and personality.

As members of the Inaugural Finance Committee, we took part in many of the inaugural activities, including the Bipartisan Dinner, and other formal events, and a People's Ball hosted at the downtown Marriott by a member of our church who wanted to throw a party for anyone and everyone to attend, whether or not they had fancy clothes to wear. It was quite a week to be in the nation's capital; there was a palpable sense of excitement and anticipation unlike anything I had experienced before, in all the years I had moved in and around the city.

James and I also got to be part of the inauguration ceremony itself, sitting close to the front on the National Mall. Wrapped up warm in our seats, the coldest January week in the capital in many years could not put a chill on things for me. I felt overwhelming pride to have Barack Obama as my President and Michelle Obama as my First Lady, and I was living my dream for our country through them.

In addition to seeing the Obamas in their professional capacities, I also witnessed a more personal side of them when they attended Alfred Street Baptist Church, sharing a pew with them on one of their occasional visits. Having the opportunity to embrace Mrs. Obama and sit down to tea with her, I saw firsthand how, despite the demands of their position, and the heights that they had reached, they remained such genuine, down-to-earth people.

Our sense of excitement did not fade once President Obama was in office. We were active in President Obama's re-election campaign, and equally delighted to celebrate his return to the White House.

While the election of America's first Black President was a watershed moment, there is a lot more work still to be done. The years since the Obamas vacated the White House have shown that, for all the advances that have been made, much remains to be addressed.

Given the disappointments that have followed those years of euphoria, it would be easy to become negative and cynical. But I choose not to. Although our country continues to struggle with big issues to do with race, equality, gender, and justice, I remain positive and optimistic. I do not believe I am being naive in doing so. I don't believe my grandchildren's lives will be effortless and free from prejudice. However, I hold a sincere expectation that their paths will be far easier than mine was, and that while their color will always be part of their identity, it won't define it.

Just looking back over my own lifetime reminds me how much progress has been made. In areas like education, employment, and social programs, there have been marked improvements for people. I do not believe that those who would prefer a return to the

America of my childhood, when the Ku Klux Klan marched with impunity, will prevail.

For many in my generation, the idea of a Black family in the White House was a distant dream. For my daughter's generation, it has become a matter of fact. I hope that by opening the door to that reality, the Obamas have paved the way for me to see another qualified Black man—or woman—achieve that goal again during my lifetime.

As I am able, I want to be part of seeing that happen. Having entered the political arena late in life, I believe I have a responsibility to continue to contribute to improving our country and the world. If I am ever tempted to think it's something to be left to others, I only have to step out onto the terrace of our Alexandria home, on the banks of the Potomac. As I look upriver some miles, I can see the dome of the Capitol in the distance, with the Lincoln Memorial nearby, a testimony to our government "of the people, by the people, for the people."

I am reminded not only of both my years serving my government, and the opportunity I had to serve my President and First Lady, but also the potential in a country in which it was possible for me to rise above my early circumstances. Imperfect as America may yet be, I believe in our better nature, and look hopefully for a fuller expression of it for all of us, regardless of race, religion, gender, ethnicity, or other identity.

•••

I was so proud watching television as Barack Obama gave his inspired 2008 acceptance speech before almost a quarter of a million people at Grant Park in Chicago, declaring, "It's been a long time coming, but... change has come to America." But despite his eloquence, I could not take my eyes off of his wife. In my mind's eye, I saw myself and every other Black woman in America standing tall and strong on stage behind her and her husband.

In the days following the election victory, I spent hours imagining what it would be like for Mrs. Obama living in the White House, worrying about how she would shield her daughters from the constant media spotlight. She had so many roles to fill and she always seemed to handle them with grace and ease, but this would be a daunting task. To be given the opportunity to play a small part in supporting her in her position remains one of the great highlights of my life.

I learned about the First Lady's volunteer team from a friend who was part of the group responsible for handling Mrs. Obama's mail. There were about twenty of them who dealt with all the correspondence she received from across the country and around the world, and my friend suggested I apply. It was an exacting process, but in due course, I was vetted and cleared to join the First Lady's Correspondence Team.

Some of the other volunteers were retired professional women like myself. One lady flew down from New York once a week for her "shift." There were also some men and young student interns in the group, making for a diverse team. We all got along well, despite our different backgrounds.

Twice a week I would travel into the capital for a day at an undisclosed government building. Though the First Lady got nowhere near the thousands of pieces of mail her husband did, she still had a sizable mailbag. Several hundred pieces of mail came in each week, written on everything from high-end stationary to pages ripped roughly from a cheap composition book.

Obviously, the mail had already been scanned for any dangerous contents by the time it arrived on our desks, where we had to open it and determine what to do with it. Many people sent gifts as a token of their appreciation.

There were heartwarming letters telling Mrs. Obama how proud the writer was of her, and that he or she was praying for her and her family. Also, there were heartbreaking letters regarding personal finances and health-related family challenges. As I told a reporter from the *Chicago Tribune* for an article on our work, "Some make me laugh, some make me sad, so it's the full range of emotions. Some I may even go home and pray for."

On a typical day I might handle forty or more letters, reading through them and determining what to do. They might be earmarked to receive a formal letter of appreciation from the First Lady's office, or if on the rare occasion the content raised causes for concern, we would need to refer it on to the Secret Service. We also kept an eye out for any letters that related to one of Mrs. Obama's special areas of interest, which included assistance for military families. Through her Joining Forces initiative, she championed education, employment, and wellness help for service members, veterans and their families. As a result, any time we heard from a military family that was seeking some kind of help, that made its way to the top of one of the piles. Some would be selected for her to respond to personally.

Those days remain some of the most rewarding and fulfilling of my life. I hold it as a great privilege to have been able to give back and support the First Lady in this way, and consider having the opportunity to serve in this way, behind the scenes, reward enough. However, the honor was made even sweeter by the manner in which Mrs. Obama showed her appreciation for what we were doing. From time to time, she would appear at the offices in which we worked, walking through to say hello and thank us. Two or three times a year, she would host some kind of a thank-you reception at the White House.

I considered this to be a special honor, though I had been there previously with James. Through his work, we had been guests at several White House events when George W. Bush was President, meeting him briefly on a number of occasions. Those visits to the home of our country's president had been memorable in their own way, of course, but somehow nothing like the invitations I received from Mrs. Obama.

With her, there would be afternoon tea, with tasty snacks served on elegant chinaware, in one of the White House's fine rooms. Mrs. Obama would thank us all as a group for what we did, and then take a few moments to visit individually, offering a hug and a smile. Even with a busy calendar of events and commitments, she never seemed rushed. Like her husband, she had a gift for making you feel seen, heard, and valued.

It was interesting to observe how much smaller Mrs. Obama, in particular, seemed in real-life than she did on television. They say that the camera makes you appear larger than you are, but I believe it was more to do with the way her personality shone through. Her quiet dignity and grace and warmth made such an emphatic statement even when she did not speak any words.

On occasions, Mrs. Obama would also invite us to participate in other White House events. These might involve being part of an entourage to welcome heads of state and other dignitaries from other countries. One time I was there as part of a receiving group for Angela

Merkel, the Chancellor of Germany. It was strange to think that their initial impression of America included meeting ordinary people like me at the White House. From my Cinderella childhood in Mulga, I had been invited to the ball!

CHAPTER TEN

ONE PART OF my family reunion, probably the single most meaningful, did not occur until many years after we siblings started to reconnect. In time, I found Momma.

She had always been a part of my life. I drew daily strength from seeing her face in the one photo I had of her, displayed in our home. And I was warmed by learning how, unconsciously, I had absorbed some of her ways; my sisters remarked on how I was so like her in ensuring that my hair and makeup were just right before starting the day. Their observation also caused some sadness. It made me realize how significant a mother is in her children's life, even when they are not aware of it. I wonder what more I may have learned from her had she lived longer.

My sisters' comment makes me feel like I catch a glimpse of Momma in the bathroom mirror each morning, not only in the facial resemblance I am glad for, but also in the way I echo her daily habit of preparing for the day. It is a sweet thought that I have unconsciously inherited some of her ways and also, I hope, some of her spirit and personality, and her heart. I wish that she had lived to see how my life turned out, and that she had gotten to see her granddaughter and even great-grandsons. I know that she would have been very proud, had she done so.

Though the grief of loss is always with a person in some way, as best I knew I was at peace with my mother's passing. I learned differently, however, one day in 2016 when I was participating in a women's Bible study group at our church. At this gathering, we were asked, "Have you done what God inspired you to do?"

The question was intriguing, and I spent some time thinking and praying about it. Was there something specific that God wanted me to do? The answer came out of the blue, something that would never have occurred to me but which presented itself with such exceptional clarity that I knew beyond any shadow of a doubt that God was speaking to me.

Go to your mother's grave.

My mind went back to the last time I was there—the cold, gray day she had been buried. All I could remember was that the cemetery had been somewhere close to a road.

Now I was on a mission. First, I contacted my siblings, but none of them had even visited Momma's grave since the funeral, nor could they remember where it was. This didn't discourage me though; somehow I just knew that I was going to find her.

In fact, it took just one more call. I knew that she had been buried not far from where we lived, so I Googled "funeral homes, Brighton, Alabama" and called the number that came up. I explained my situation, that I was looking for a cemetery in the area but all I could remember was that it was located by a main street, and that we'd driven up on part of the property with the hearse.

"Oh, I know where you are talking about," the woman said immediately. "You mean New Oak Dale Cemetery." She gave me the name and number of the man responsible for the facility.

He was equally helpful. He said that he would need to check the records and came back to me a couple of days later to confirm that, yes, my mother lay there. She was in an old section of the cemetery to the rear, he told me. James and I immediately made plans to visit, taking Emma along with us and meeting up with Frankie who for many years had lived only ten miles or so from where our mother was buried.

The cemetery workers had cleaned up her plot by the time we arrived, but it was unadorned: no headstone, no marking of any kind, just a flat piece of grassy ground, partly in the shade of a mulberry tree. I felt a rush of mixed emotions as I stood there on the plain ground—great delight that I had found her and deep sorrow to think of all the years she had been there unidentified, unnoticed, unremembered. But most of all I had this sense of joy, that by coming we were somehow validating her life.

We each stood there silently with our own thoughts. In my head, I told Momma how much I loved her and how grateful I had been to be her daughter. I told her how sorry I was that her life had been so hard and that she had been treated so poorly. I told her that I still missed her, but I was doing okay, and life was good. I told her that I wished we had known each other better, and how I was sure that we would have enjoyed the same loving relationship I had with Ashley. And, I told her, I would be back to visit.

After about an hour there, the caretaker who had helped us find the grave came over as we finished. He led us in a prayer, and I put the flowers I had brought on the ground as a sort of deposit, guaranteeing my return. I walked back to our car with a full heart, smiling through tears.

Leaving the cemetery this time was very different than the previous time, more than half a century earlier. Then I had been a bewildered nine-year-old, helpless and hopeless, caught in a storm beyond my control. Now I was a much more confident woman, finally realizing a sense of deep peace that had eluded me for a long time. Above all, I was so grateful to God, that He knew there was this missing piece in my life that had to be found and placed, like completing a puzzle.

Now that we knew where our mother lay, we wanted to be sure that she was honored. Frankie worked as a contractor, so he was able to arrange for a slab to be laid on the plot, and later we ordered a headstone. We chose a simple inscription: "Mama. Forever in Our Heart."

Sarah joined the rest of us when we went to dedicate it, on a bright sunny afternoon on January 14, 2017. We took a portable CD player with us and played "Amazing Grace," and said prayers of remembrance. Now each time we return to the area to visit family or when we return to Alabama State for some event, we make a point to drive out to the cemetery to refresh the flowers on her grave and spend a few moments in grateful silence.

People sometimes talk about events like these as bringing "closure," as though it signifies the shutting of a door, the closing of something. For me, finding where my mother was buried in some ways meant the opposite. Having discovered where she lay, part of me now wanted to learn how she got there. I floated the idea of having Momma's body exhumed and an autopsy performed, but my siblings did not want to go down that rocky road.

I decided to let it go and leave all of that in God's hands. He knows all the facts, and I will learn them when I am reunited with Momma one day in heaven, where the Bible tells us there will be no more tears, no more mourning and crying, and whatever happened will not matter any more. I choose just to be grateful for finding her, which has allowed me to reconnect with a part of my life that had been lost, somehow making what I have now all the sweeter.

• • •

THAT GRAVE EPISODE was a gift from God in more ways than one. Not only did it allow me to find and honor my mother in a way that has been so meaningful, but it also remains one of the most profound spiritual moments of my life. I knew without question that God was speaking directly and personally to me. I knew that in telling me to find my mother's grave He was not only saying that she mattered, but also that I mattered—that it was important to Him that she be remembered and equally that I be comforted through the process. It is moving to think that God cares about each of us so much.

My faith has been a comfort and a source of strength to me as long as I can remember. Even before I made my twice-repeated steps down to the mourner's bench, I had a sense of Him as being kind and benevolent, if a little distant. Though after Momma's death our house had been swept clean of affection, when I went to church on Sundays and heard the people raising their voices in song and in prayer, I just knew that God loved me, and for the time being that was enough.

Claiming Jesus as my own was, of course, another milestone on my journey of faith. Having had it pummeled into me by my stepmother that I was a terrible person, I knew desperately that I needed saving, and I could not get over how unfair it was that Jesus, who had done no wrong, should suffer so that we might be forgiven. It was such a comfort to know that, although I might not have been accepted by Daddy and my stepmother, I was accepted by God. There was someone there who cared about me. I may not have known where my siblings were, but I had not been left all alone.

Our childhood experiences affect how we see and understand God. Some of those memories evaporate over time while others can linger and resist being cast away. Looking back, I am more aware now of how all that played out in my life. With my stepmother's constant hammering of how bad I was, I had no question that I was a sinner in need of a Savior, that's for sure! Even after going to the mourner's bench, I'd ask Him to help make me better, so that I might somehow please my stepmother.

While I loved Jesus, the idea of God as Father was understandably more remote; after all, my earthly father had been cold and cruel. Though I have overcome some of the hurdles that stood in my way over the years as a result of my difficult childhood, my greatest ongoing challenge in life has been finding a way to trust in God when things seem hopeless or when I have been at my wit's end about how to solve a problem.

I'm sure that a big part of this stemmed from the extreme physical and emotional abuse I suffered as a child. Until I learned to let it go, those experiences affected every experience—positive or negative—and prevented me from warmly embracing and celebrating my blessings. Constantly waiting for the other shoe to drop, unable to enjoy the many good things that happen in life, is a dispiriting way to live.

The doubts started to fester when I was a young girl filled with questions. First and foremost: Why did my mother have to die? And then, what had I done to deserve the disdain of my stepmother, other than to reach out to her for affection? As a teenager, that insecurity grew into massive doubts about my appearance. For a natural introvert, such uncertainties only reinforced my tendency to withdraw, making me wary of things and people I did not understand, and generally fretful about the unknown.

As I matured, my confidence in some areas blossomed, but I was never fully able to rid myself of my doubts. The questions that had plagued me remained, and that left me fearful and insecure. The person I saw in the mirror was not the person I knew myself to be, but I wasn't entirely sure who I was. If I couldn't forge an identity in my own mind, how could I expect other people to understand me?

The view in the mirror was inaccurate but I couldn't see the "real me." Instead I saw blemishes that didn't exist. Indeed, nearly my whole self-image was composed of things that were not true, and as a result, for most of my adult life I felt inadequate in both professional and social environments, though I made sure not to show it. I allowed the horrors of my childhood to strip me of my confidence, self-esteem, and joy. Rather than viewing myself as a victim of horrible circumstances, I saw my mistreatment as a sign of personal failure.

Consequently, I believed that I was never good enough for the next job—even as my career advancements should have signaled otherwise. My perceived inadequacies caused many sleepless nights and led to turbulent days as I struggled to keep my head above water. Subconsciously, I feared failing and focused on what I did not have instead of what I did have.

As my relationship with Jesus grew stronger in the subsequent years, memories of my childhood grew less painful. I never completely put the bad times out of my mind, but I found increasingly that I could use them as a source of strength rather than as a reason to despair. Years later, I woke next to James one morning with an almost euphoric sense of relief bubbling up inside me. It was as if I had gone to sleep with a tremendous pressure on my chest and awakened light as a feather, all of that previous weight having evaporated.

Coincidentally, the first thing that caught my eye as I looked across the room was a family picture that typically reminded me of my childhood and my stepmother's dark, hateful eyes. My usual reaction was one of anger. But not this morning—somehow, I felt nothing but forgiveness and relief. God had given me the ability to compartmentalize the horrors of my childhood in one small corner of my brain and refill the space that they had previously occupied with nothing but light and joy. It was an absolute gift, one that I cherish to this day.

· · ·

WITH ALL THE healing, hope, and happiness God brought into my life through the years, the time when as a young girl I had asked Him to take my life seemed like a distant memory. Until one spring day in 2005 when I woke and moved to get out of bed.

I was overwhelmed by excruciating pain from head to toe. It started in the center of my back and seemed to radiate out in waves through the rest of my body, leaving me almost gasping for breath. When I tried to move my head, it felt like my neck was on fire. I tried to sit up and my back felt even worse. Maybe I had tweaked a muscle, I thought: the previous day I had been working on some new floor exercises at the gym with my personal trainer.

It quickly became clear that this was more than a localized injury. When I finally mustered the strength to swing my legs out of the bed onto the floor, the same harsh pain shot through my knees, too. I knew I'd done nothing that might have led directly to these problems; I'd never been a runner or overexerted myself athletically in a manner that would have taxed my legs. Nor had I been lifting weights. Where was all of this pain coming from?

I sat back down and mentally ran through my personal medical history. The overall picture was one of good health. Other than for the occasional runny nose or nagging cough as the result of a simple cold, I'd always been pretty healthy. I had gotten sick in college, once, when the doctor told me that the pericardial sac around my heart was inflamed, but that issue had resolved itself fairly quickly, and it was the last major illness that I'd suffered.

Beyond that, I hadn't had any major sicknesses in my life. Not that I had been one hundred percent healthy, though. In my forties I developed fibroid tumors, a condition not uncommon for women of color. When my doctor first identified them, he suggested a wait-and-see policy which I questioned but went along with, sadly resulting in a partial hysterectomy at the age of forty-two.

Now, as I sat on the side of the bed a decade later, it felt like I was starting the first day of the rest of my life as an impaired senior citizen, even though up until then I certainly hadn't considered myself to be aging. I had been an active member of my community, playing tennis and participating in church activities. Having been fortunate enough to have been able to conclude my government service while still relatively young, I had been looking forward to an active retirement. This interruption threw those plans into disarray.

Life has certainly changed in many ways since then, going through each day in chronic pain but with no clear answer. Like my father, I have developed a severe and chronic form of arthritis, with no expectation that it will ever get better. Some nights I'll be fast asleep, only for a jolting pain to lift me from the bed, like a charley horse on steroids. Frequently broken sleep only adds to the overall discomfort, making me constantly tired.

We have consulted some of the top doctors in the Washington, DC, area and they have all seemingly come up with different diagnoses—among them cervical facet joint syndrome, myofascial pain syndrome, cervicalgia, and cervical spondylosis. They have recommended treatment regimens including injections in my spine, prescription pain medications—including a period on opioids, which the doctor advised I stop taking to avoid becoming fully addicted—and physical therapy, acupuncture, and the services of a chiropractor. Despite hundreds of hours of effort, and mountains of resources spent to find a cure, the constant pain remains. I wear a pain patch each and every day, which brings a small measure of relief.

The physical discomfort is horrible, but at least I can continue being active, and I work with my trainer to slow its advancement. Strengthening my muscles and attempting to keep good posture helps. I aim to get in ten thousand steps a day to keep my blood flowing well and my circulation good. I am doing all I can to alleviate the symptoms.

On the other hand, there has been nothing I can do about what at first was identified as a side effect of the unremitting physical distress—the ever-increasing impairment of both my memory and my attention span. However, after numerous tests and evaluations, my neurologist delivered the disheartening news that I have the early onset of Alzheimer's Disease. It has been some some small comfort to discover that my back pain and memory loss were unrelated, but my frustration is still extreme.

Becoming more and more forgetful is especially debilitating and traumatic for someone who has always been an exceptionally detail-oriented person. I thrived on knowing all of the facts and figures about anything that concerned me, and now there are days when I walk just a few blocks from home and have to call James to guide me back because I cannot remember the way, though I have taken that same route countless times.

On one occasion, I visited a spa not far from my home, an area I'd visited hundreds—if not thousands—of times, and when I emerged from my treatments I had no idea where I was. I walked the whole area looking for my car but couldn't find it. It was such a helpless feeling.

In order to help me remember to take my daily medication, I purchased a pill box that reveals whether that day's medication has been removed. James makes sure it is kept filled appropriately. Unfortunately, there have been a few times that I have removed my meds from the pill box and discovered later that day that I had not gotten round to taking them. A simple pill box is too much to handle for someone who used to manipulate huge spreadsheets and data files!

I have learned to develop little helping skills. If I am going to drive somewhere on my own—which is an increasingly rare thing—when I park, I will write down where the vehicle is located so I can find my way back. I also set a series of reminders on my phone if I need to do something—one that the time is coming up, another when the moment arrives, and a follow-up for later in case I somehow still forget.

Even at home, in my most familiar surroundings, it can take me ten minutes to remember where I just put something down. James has said that, at times, it is as though I am a visitor in my own home. Once, I was baking a pie and forgot that I put it in the oven, so it burned. These days James handles all the kitchen duties. Losing the ability to read books has been frustrating, but I find that I can follow audiobooks, so that has been some comfort.

The result of this memory loss has been to cause me to withdraw. For many years, I was very active in our church, even serving as Vice Chair of the Board of Trustees. I'm now more of a pew-warmer, and I have also pulled back from social settings. It took me many years to overcome my early awkwardness, but eventually I came to a place where I felt comfortable in those environments; sadly, now I feel inadequate in even basic conversations because I can't remember names or what I said just a few moments ago, let alone what happened years past.

One time, I was speaking to a group of high school students in Alexandria about how they could prepare for their futures (as I had on a number of previous occasions), when I completely lost my train of thought. I had given the same presentation a number of times, but I simply could not remember what was next. My mind was completely blank. I froze for a moment before James, who was sitting in the audience, called out the next point in my presentation, and I was able to pick up where I had gotten lost and complete what I had to say. But I knew as I left the stage that my public speaking days were over. Now, sometimes even the simplest words will escape me. While I can remember faces, often the names that go with them elude me.

All this has triggered extreme depression at times, and I've sought treatment for that, too. There have even been moments during this long, arduous season when I have, just for a moment, again thought that it might be good if God could just take me home, as I did when I was a lonely girl. What value do I have, I sometimes wonder?

Two things bring me out of that—well, actually three. First is my hope and faith in God, who has already brought me through so much in life, and who I believe loves and cares for me even when I don't understand what is happening. And then my two beautiful grandsons, Sebastian and Xavier, who bring such delight to James and me. I don't want to miss a moment of watching them grow.

Becoming a grandmother has been a dream come true, but with its own sweet kind of pain, because playing with the boys and holding them aggravates my physical condition. How cruel it seems that the thing that I love to do most causes such hurt.

One person with whom I have shared some of the difficulties of this ongoing physical challenge said that I seemed like a swan—poised and graceful above the waterline, but beneath the surface paddling hard to make any progress. I fear that makes me sound more noble than I deserve. While I know that James, Ashley, and Damian do not resent helping me out when needed, I find it hard not to feel like I am a burden, and that is very difficult to come to terms with for someone who has long prided herself on being self-sufficient and capable. So as part of not wanting to impose on others, I always try to put on a brave face so that people do not know that I am in considerable discomfort all my waking hours.

It is also difficult for me to have to rely on James as much as I do. He never complains and has adjusted his life to be there for me. Knowing how much he enjoyed the way we would discuss things, I know he finds it hard when I am so forgetful, sometimes asking him the same thing several times within just a few minutes.

One regret is that my situation has curtailed some of our travel. As we got older and became more established, we had enjoyed getting to explore the world together—London, Paris, and Venice are three of our favorite cities. We still make some trips, but they are quite physically taxing for me these days, so I have to be careful.

In telling about all this now for the first time, I do so with some reluctance. But I hope that in sharing some of my struggles, I may be able to encourage others who may be facing some sort of similar intractable challenge in their life. I know that I have so much to be thankful for, and while the pain can be terrible, the memory loss can be tormenting, and I occasionally suffer from depression, I know that I am loved and that I still have a lot of great days ahead of me.

• • •

T<small>HOUGH</small> I <small>WAKE</small> up sad and hurting on some days, it's not enough to stop me. On one such morning, recently, I received a message directly from God, as clear as day. Just like the time He told me to go find my mother's grave, I knew without a shadow of a doubt that He had spoken to me.

It was so momentous and so uplifting that I didn't want to lose the moment. So I captured the thought as a daily reminder in my calendar. It reads, *I'm doing the best that I can. If I forget something it's okay; if people can't accept me as I am, it's okay.*

Each time I read it, my response is this: "If God said it, I believe it. Amen!"

I know that when things go wrong in my life it does not mean that God has forsaken me. I recognize that being a Christian won't always shield me from adversity, ease the pain, or heal the hurt; we all have our burdens to carry. I still do not understand everything about the way that God works, but my faith is complete.

On occasions, I have asked God to heal me. But mostly I pray that He will give me all that I need to live well in the circumstances I am facing. We don't always get all that we would like in this life, after all. Jesus certainly didn't. The night before His crucifixion, He asked God the Father to take from Him the cup of suffering He faced. God didn't, but He remained faithful to the end.

With age, I have grown wiser and my sight has grown clearer. I have learned to put my faith in Him for the long haul and not base it on short-term situations and outcomes. Looking back, I see God's hand on my life journey, starting off as a shy little girl and developing into an increasingly confident and successful woman with a loving family. When I first walked to the mourner's bench I had no idea that God would take me on the ride that I've experienced, nor could I have envisioned the amazing things that I've seen and done. But I know that God has led me where He wants me to be.

I think of the story of Joseph, sold into slavery by his brothers and later thrown into jail after being unfairly accused of wrongdoing by Potiphar's wife. Joseph languished in prison for two years before finally being released, and then elevated to a position of great influence in Egypt. Finally reunited with his brothers, they asked forgiveness for their wrongdoing. Joseph told them that while they may have acted with bad intent, "God meant it for good."

Similarly, I believe that He has worked in my life to turn around the challenging seasons I have experienced. I can't change the past, and by dwelling on it I give it power over today, so I choose not to. What's done is done. Meanwhile, worrying too much about tomorrow robs me of what I can choose to enjoy now, so I determine not to go there, either.

God has opened so many doors of wonderful blessing to me. He has brought me in from the cold of a lonely, neglected childhood to a place of warmth and acceptance in a loving family. Thanks to His strength and guidance, I know that I am more than the sum of my experiences and my difficult beginnings. He has done exceedingly and abundantly more than a little girl from Mulga, Alabama, could have ever hoped or dreamed, and I will continue to trust Him.

I am so grateful for the opportunity to write this book. I am blessed to have treasured family and friends to support me during this difficult time, and I will cope as best as I can as this disease progresses. In the meantime, I will enjoy special moments with those who are so dear to me and continue to be thankful to God for a life well lived.

ABOUT THE AUTHOR

JULIETTE MCNEIL was born in Birmingham, Alabama. She attended Alabama State University, where she earned a Bachelor of Science Degree in Accounting and Economics. Juliette had a distinguished career with the Federal Government for more than 25 years and is a retired member of the Senior Executive Service.

She began her career as a Defense Contract Auditor and was instrumental in saving the Federal Government tens of millions of dollars. She also played a pivotal role in standardizing and implementing business principles for Information Technology resources throughout the Department of Defense

(DOD). In addition, she was the first Black woman to serve as Director of Financial Management for the Environmental Protection Agency.

Juliette earned numerous awards and professional distinctions, including a Bronze Medal for commendable service. In recognition of her many contributions to the DOD, a United States flag was flown over the Pentagon in honor of her retirement.

In her private life, Juliette serves as President of the McNeil Family Foundation, through which she was a major donor to the National Museum of African American History and Culture. A former Vice Chair of the Board of Trustees at Alfred Street Baptist Church in Alexandria, Virginia, she has been active in community service, with a special interest in helping children. Juliette also served as a volunteer in First Lady Michelle Obama's Correspondence Office.

Juliette has been married to her husband, James, since 1976, and is the proud mother of Ashley, who is married and has two sons.

My father, John H. Carbin.

Momma, Vera Mae Carbin, aged about 16.

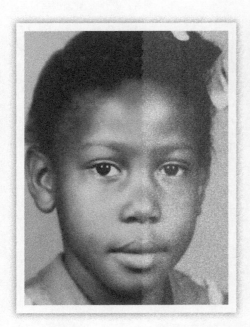

Me, aged around six or seven, with a quiet sadness in my eyes.

James and I toast each other on our wedding day, July 3, 1976, my sorority-colors dress revealing the absence of a mother's guidance.

The last time I saw my father he remained as distant as ever: with (second left to right) Sarah, Frankie, and Emma.

A happy family: with our beloved daughter, Ashley, at about 18 months.

Reunited: James and I (left) with my long-lost siblings and their spouses (left to right): Robert and Emma Brown, Frank and Sarah Wright, Frankie and Elizabeth Carbin.

A quiet moment of reflection and thanksgiving as we dedicate Momma's resting place in 2016.

A proud moment with President Barack Obama, during his 2012 re-election campaign.

With Vice President Joe Biden and his wife, Jill, at their official residence, at the start of his second term in office.

*Serving as part of First Lady Michelle Obama's correspon-
dence team (rear, fifth from left) was a very special season.*

With James McNeil, the love of my life.

CPSIA information can be obtained
at www.ICGtesting.com
Printed in the USA
LVHW091510050719
623268LV00001B/99/P

9 781950 718122